WHY
GOOD PEOPLE
DO
BAD THINGS

Also by Debbie Ford

The Dark Side of the Light Chasers

Spiritual Divorce

The Secret of the Shadow

The Right Questions

The Best Year of Your Life

WHY GOOD PEOPLE DO BAD THINGS

HOW TO STOP BEING YOUR OWN WORST ENEMY

DEBBIE FORD

HarperOne
An Imprint of HarperCollinsPublishers

This book is dedicated to my amazing family,

my loyal friends, my brilliant staff, and the

Integrative Coaches who have given me their

hearts, time, love, and energy to make

this book possible.

WHY GOOD PEOPLE DO BAD THINGS: *How to Stop Being Your Own Worst Enemy.* Copyright © 2008 by Debbie Ford. All rights reserved. Printed in the United States of America. No part of this book may be used or reproduced in any manner whatsoever without written permission except in the case of brief quotations embodied in critical articles and reviews. For information address HarperCollins Publishers, 10 East 53rd Street, New York, NY 10022.

HarperCollins books may be purchased for educational, business, or sales promotional use. For information please write: Special Markets Department, HarperCollins Publishers, 10 East 53rd Street, New York, NY 10022.

HarperCollins Web site: http://www.harpercollins.com

HarperCollins®, 📖®, and HarperOne™ are trademarks of HarperCollins Publishers.

FIRST EDITION

Library of Congress Cataloging-in-Publication Data
Ford, Debbie.
    Why good people do bad things : how to stop being your own worst enemy / Debbie Ford. — 1st ed.
        p.   cm.
    ISBN 978–0–06–089737–6
    1. Self-defeating behavior.   2. Stupidity.   3. Errors.   4. Self-actualization (Psychology)   I. Title.
    BF637.S37F67   2008
    158.1—dc22   2007035993

08 09 10 11 12   RRD(H)   10 9 8 7 6 5 4 3 2 1

CONTENTS

The Guest House

This being human is a guest house.
Every morning a new arrival.
A joy, a depression, a meanness,
some momentary awareness comes
as an unexpected visitor.

Welcome and entertain them all!
Even if they're a crowd of sorrows,
who violently sweep your house
empty of its furniture,
still treat each guest honorably.
He may be clearing you out
for some new delight.

The dark thought, the shame, the malice,
meet them at the door laughing,
and invite them in.

Be grateful for whoever comes,
because each has been sent
as a guide from beyond.

—Rumi; translation by Coleman Barks

A NOTE TO THE READER

Exploring why good people do bad things and why we turn into our own worst enemies is one of the most intense inquiries that any of us will ever embark upon. It is an eye-opening expedition to uncover the vast and often hidden darkness that influences our choices and pervades every facet of our human experience. This journey will take us into the heart of the duality of darkness and light that operates within each one of us. It's a challenging yet compelling conversation because most of us are blind to the whole of who we are. We go to great lengths to continue to see the world through the perspectives we are familiar with and will do whatever we deem necessary to protect the person we believe ourselves to be—whether good or bad. That is why this inquiry requires us to step outside what we have long held to be the truth about ourselves and expose the hidden mechanisms that drive us to hurt ourselves and other people.

This investigation into the polarities, ambiguities, and hypocrisies of our humanity demands that we bring radical honesty to the places where we've been in denial, that we bring compassion to the parts of ourselves we've been ashamed of, and that we bring courage to the areas of our lives where we've been afraid to admit our vulnerabilities. It's not a process of smoothing over, covering up, or pretending that the things we do to harm ourselves and others are not that big a deal. It's a process that forces us to stop minimizing the impact of our self-destructive behaviors; admit what they are costing us and how they lead us to becoming our own worst enemy. To stop our self-sabotage we must be self-confronting and willing to understand how the primal split from our authentic nature caused us to create a fabricated self—what I refer to throughout this book as the *false self*. Our false self is the culprit that causes us to act out in inappropriate ways, destroy our relationships, sabotage our dreams, and place ourselves in harm's way.

This path from darkness to light, from emotional pain to spiritual liberation, has been my journey for the past twenty-five years, and yet even after writing five previous books I am still aware of a deeper truth that I have yet to share. My goal with this book is to have you understand that your deepest pain arises as a result of the primal split between your higher nature and your human self. My intention is to lovingly support you in unraveling the lies and distortions, the guilt and the shame, that unwittingly turn you into your own worst enemy. I want to interrupt the internal mechanisms that cause you to turn your back on yourself, ignore your intuition, inappropriately cross boundaries, and give your power away to some person, thought, belief, addiction, or impulse that might lead you down a dark road to nowhere rather than the liberated path you were meant to travel. The information and processes you will find in this book will allow you to heal your deepest regrets, challenge your insecurities, befriend your self-doubts, confront your inner demons, and face up to the ways in which you participate in your own self-destruction.

This book will provide you with a reliable path to defy the gravitational pull of your past and step into the infinite possibilities of your true and limitless self.

I know that the greatest gift I can give you is the benefit of all my experience as a workshop leader, coach, and educator. After struggling with my own darkness and destructive tendencies, I have come to understand the absolute perfection and absurdity of the human experience. I know the power, as well as the potential hazards, of our unprocessed pain. And I know what it takes to make peace with the past and integrate the unresolved conflicts of our conscious and unconscious minds. My absolute faith that the gold lies in the dark is what allowed me to heal my shame and help hundreds of thousands of other people heal theirs. It was my own journey through darkness that helped me build an intimate relationship with my authentic nature. It was not my good self but rather my evil twin that led me to heal my emotional wounds and ultimately launched my career. It's not my quick wit or my perceived brilliance that has allowed me to transform the lives of hundreds of thousands of people, but rather the wisdom I gained as a result of integrating my anger, discontent, shame, fear, and insecurities. In fact, it was my inability to function well in the world that forced me to strengthen my spiritual connection and learn how to thrive, even after devastation. It is the very darkness that I didn't want to be or experience that has driven me to become the woman I always longed to be.

All of my flaws and negative qualities—of which I have many—have brought me priceless gifts, for they are what have led me to become who I am today. I can no longer stand in judgment or disapproval of my human flaws, weaknesses, and dark impulses, because the integration and wisdom of my own humanity are what have led me to deliver my greatest gift and create a life beyond what I could ever have imagined for myself. Because of this, I believe I am the perfect person to guide and support you in understanding who you are and why you do the things you do.

When we come to understand that we are all both good and bad, light and dark, strong and weak, brilliant and oftentimes utterly stupid, we begin the profound process of healing the internal split that invariably takes place for most of us at some time in our lives. This is the only path I've found that actually relieves human suffering. We achieve peace not by learning new tricks or more strategies to hide our imperfections but by embracing more of our insecurities, more of our shame, our fear, and our vulnerabilities. When we heal the split between our darkness and our light, our Dr. Jekyll and Mr. Hyde, we have the resources to make better choices, think more empowering thoughts, and behave in ways that leave us feeling proud and inspired. We gain the courage and the confidence to see things exactly as they are, without any self-deception or illusion, and we understand that it is not by accident that each of us becomes the person we are today or that we struggle with the issues that we are faced with. With this priceless information in hand, we hold the key to unlocking our tendency toward self-sabotage, and we open up the door to living a life beyond the limitations of our false self—a life filled with passion, meaning, and purpose; a life graced by the very experiences and heartaches that brought us to our knees.

PART ONE

THE NEVER-ENDING BATTLE

1

THE BEACH-BALL
EFFECT

Why Good People Do Bad Things is a powerful inquiry into the hidden forces that drive us to commit unbelievable acts of self-sabotage and self-destruction. We've all heard the stories; they show up on the evening news, on the front page of newspapers, and as headlines in the weekly tabloids: the Olympic sports hero who falls from grace after being accused of injecting steroids; the TV evangelist who gets arrested for soliciting prostitutes; the schoolteacher who carries on an affair with one of her students; or the baseball star who gambles on his own games. These are the public demonstrations of good people who have gone astray, and they have become our national obsession.

But countless other acts of self-destruction and unthinkable acts of cruelty take place, unbeknownst to us, in our own backyards: the successful eye surgeon who gambles his kids' college tuition away; the public official who takes a bribe; the PTA mom who is having an affair with her best friend's husband; the hospital administrator who commits insurance fraud; or the financial manager who embezzles money from his clients. These are people whom most of their peers would consider good people, not common criminals, psychopaths, or sociopaths whose histories might predict their unscrupulous behavior. These are people like you and me, people who started out with big dreams for their future. But despite their good intentions, these so-called good people did some very bad things, most often without even understanding why.

Our society is rampant with acts of self-destruction that leave most of us perplexed and asking, "Why did he or she do that? Why did I do this? How could this happen?" Self-sabotage is the proverbial hammer over the head that finally wakes us up, demanding that we pay attention. For most of us, it takes something devastating to crack us open, to get us out of our minds and into our hearts. It takes the pain of a broken heart and shattered dreams to push us beyond the limited realities we have created for ourselves.

We are spiritual beings whether we want to admit it or not, and inherent in our DNA is a design to return us home—home to our true essence, our greatest self, our limitless self. One of the ways we unconsciously ensure our return is through pain. Pain is the greatest motivator for change. It is the spiritual crowbar that pries open the door to new realities. Would we look into our deeper selves, dwell in them, grapple with them, inquire into them, and initiate change in our lives if everything was perfect? More than likely we would just continue living day by day in the comfort of our familiar worlds.

Self-sabotage is a catalyst that can change our world in an instant. We can go from arrogant and blind to humble and open—in just a matter of seconds. The pain we cause ourselves is a tremendous spiritual gift. When explored and understood for its true purpose, the pain of our own self-sabotage reveals new and uncharted territories that can change the course of our lives.

The Underbelly of the Human Psyche

The underbelly of the human psyche, what is often referred to as our dark side, is the origin of every act of self-sabotage. Birthed out of shame, fear, and denial, it misdirects our good intentions and drives us to unthinkable acts of self-destruction and not-so-unbelievable acts of self-sabotage.

Shame and denial feed our dark side for one simple reason. If we accepted our weaknesses, flaws, and shortcomings as a natural part of our humanity, we would have the ability to ask for help when we are confronted with an impulse that we don't know how to deal with. We would recognize that these dark impulses—such as the urge to have sex with people other than our spouse, to take money that doesn't belong to us, or to lie in order to better position ourselves—are a natural part of our humanity that needs to be understood and embraced. But because these urges are left unexplored and unexamined, they get wrapped in shame and denial and kept hidden in the dark. And it is there that our shadow self, the unwanted and denied aspects of ourselves, gathers more power until a blowup is inevitable.

Every aspect of ourselves that we've denied, every thought and feeling that we've deemed unacceptable and wrong, eventually makes itself known in our lives. When we are busy building a business, creating a family, or taking care of those we love, when we are too busy to pay attention to our emotions, we have to hide our dark impulses and shame-filled qualities, which leaves us at risk for an external explosion. In a matter of minutes, when we least expect it, a rejected or unwanted aspect of ourselves can pop up and destroy our lives, our reputations, and all of our hard work. This is what I call the Beach-Ball Effect.

Think of the amount of energy it takes to hold an inflated beach ball underwater for an extended period of time. The moment you relax or take your attention away from keeping it submerged, the ball will bounce back up and splash water in your face. The Beach-Ball Effect is at work when you have suppressed something deep within your psyche, stored it in the recesses of your subconscious, and then, just when you think everything is going your way, something happens: You send a slanderous e-mail to the wrong colleague. You get lured into betraying someone you love for a night of meaningless passion. You get behind the wheel of a car after having three drinks and get arrested for drunk driving. You get caught dipping into your family's trust fund. You fly off into a rage in front of your new lover. You make an inappropriate comment that costs you your job. You blow an important deadline right before your big review. You haul off and hit your child in a moment of frustration. . . . In other words, the beach ball—your repressed urges and your unprocessed pain—pops up and hits you in the face, sabotaging your dreams, robbing you of your dignity, and leaving you drenched in shame.

How many more blatant acts of self-sabotage do we have to witness to understand the devastating effects of denying and suppressing our unprocessed emotional garbage? Don Imus is a perfect example. Here is a man who worked hard to become one of biggest radio and TV celebrities in the country over the course of thirty-five years—his entire career was based on communication. And in less than one minute the reputation he had spent years building was destroyed. The beach ball bounced up and hit him in the face.

Mel Gibson built the persona of someone who takes a moral and ethical stand for others and creates movies with strong spiritual messages. And although he vehemently denied accusations of anti-Semitism in his movie *The Passion of the Christ,* in one drunken tirade the attitudes and beliefs that were hidden in his shadow couldn't be held down. When pulled over and arrested for driving under the influence, he shamed himself with a barrage of outrageous statements.

There are countless ways for the beach ball to pop up and smack us back into reality. It could be something as small as picking a fight with your husband right before you are about to go out on a long-overdue date, or criticizing your child in front of her friends after spending months trying to build her trust. It might be procrastinating on updating your résumé and missing a huge opportunity, or spending a night in front of the refrigerator after dieting for three months. Maybe it manifests itself as oversleeping and missing your best friend's bridal shower or calling your lover by the wrong name. Maybe it's making a smart-ass comment to yourself while thinking someone had already hung up the phone when actually they had not. As long as we are unwilling to look at the beach balls that are lying just beneath the surface of our consciousness, we will unknowingly have to live in fear of the moment they will pop up and the effects they will have on our lives and the lives of others when they do. And believe me, it is a rare case when we are the only ones who get hurt; more often than not, our unprocessed pain will hurt many people. Many lives will be inconvenienced, many hearts will be broken, and some nearby innocent spectators will get caught in the splash.

Let's think of our suppressed emotions and disowned qualities as human lava. Lava exists beneath the surface of the earth. If there are no steam vents at the earth's surface to release the pressure of the powerful force that lies beneath, its only outlet comes in the form of an eruption. Likewise, within our psyches our dark urges and impulses build up, and unless we find safe, healthy ways to release them, they express themselves in inappropriate and potentially dangerous ways. By acknowledging, accepting, and embracing our dark side, we create natural steam vents within ourselves. By providing an opening, we eliminate the worry about an explosion because we are allowing the pressure to be released in a safe and appropriate way. But when it is concealed in darkness, repressed out of shame, and denied out of fear, the shadow has no choice but to erupt. The mental and emotional outpouring that follows has less to do with our circumstances and who is around us than it does with our need to release the pressure.

Our psyches naturally seek a release from the internal pressure caused by the repression of the disowned aspects of ourselves. This is why we are so obsessed with bad news, bad behavior, and especially the media's stories that exploit the downfall of people who are at the top of their game. Each time we hear one of these shocking tales of greed, lust, perversion, stupidity, deceit, or betrayal, we unconsciously get some internal release and relief from the pressure of our own dark side. When we see someone famous who is accused of molesting a thirteen-year-old boy, suddenly our own fascination with porn seems to pale in comparison. When our city councilwoman is caught shoplifting, cheating on our taxes seems insignificant. This obsession with darkness and failure in the media allows us to take momentary shelter in the hope that we are not as horrible as those we see portrayed around us. Yet our fascination with their darkness tells a different story.

Consider the proliferation of reality television shows that allow us to voyeuristically observe the competitive, petty, and often mean-spirited behavior of the colorful cast of characters. We would not be so intrigued, so engrossed, and so compelled if we did not possess the same urges and instincts. When we are projecting onto others and judging their behaviors, our own suddenly don't seem that bad. Sometimes we look to the dark side of those around us for a sense of camaraderie and belonging. We see their shadow, and at some unconscious level we feel relieved that we are not the only ones who are acting out in that way.

If we want to ensure that our dark side does not become the driving force behind our actions, we must first unravel the inner workings of our human operating system: what's included in the hard wiring, built in to every human being, and what is added on later as the software that gets programmed into each one of us. We must expose the two contradictory forces that exist within each of us: the force that compels us to expand our ability to give and receive love, to heed our inner voice and be a contributing member of our community—and the force that holds us back, sabotages our best efforts, and repeatedly steers us in a direction that is inconsistent with our highest goals and deepest values. This is the time to open our eyes to why good people—hardworking, committed, well-meaning, churchgoing, contributory people—do bad things; and to look with honest eyes at how we become our own worst enemy.

2

THE SPLIT

W hy will some of us sacrifice our deepest desires, our dignity, and our dreams to satisfy an impulse that can destroy our lives and the lives of those around us? To understand why good people do bad things, we must begin by understanding the basic structure of our humanity, the psychology of the ego, and the duality that exists within every person on the planet. Acknowledging what it is to be a human being is a fundamental step in healing the split between the light and the dark. If we don't understand the flaws and weaknesses of the human machine as well as its perfection and strengths, we will never be able to make peace within ourselves or end the internal war that has us commit outrageous acts of self-sabotage and suffer needlessly over the repetitive bad behaviors that ransack our lives.

Why must we acknowledge and understand the duality that exists within each of us? Because it is not our true self that takes us down the dark roads that rob of us of our dignity and self-respect. It is not our more evolved self that sabotages our success and drags us through humiliation and pain. It is in fact our wounded self, the part of us that is filled with hidden insecurities and shame. The wounded ego is the aspect of our humanity that by its very design is vulnerable to our darkest impulses and has the ability to wipe out our hard work and obliterate our dreams. It is the wounded human ego and the shadowy dark forces that lurk beneath the surface of our conscious minds that hold the power to ruin our lives in an instant or drag us through a painful existence filled with failed relationships, bad business deals, disappointing outcomes, and stupid mistakes.

It is our shame-based personas and all the shadows that lie beneath the surface of our conscious awareness that make us "good people" do bad things. Our false self is directed by our misguided whims, our unmet needs, and our deep feelings of unworthiness. It seeks gain at any cost and goes after outer fulfillment to cover up the emotional emptiness that lies beneath the faces that we show the world. It is the false self, birthed out of our woundedness, our deep insecurities, and our self-loathing, that must get addressed if we are to befriend ourselves and ensure a stable future. And if we are unwilling to even acknowledge the existence of this wounded false self, how can we begin to heal it, let alone befriend it?

A Spiritual Problem

In essence, why good people do bad things is a spiritual problem that arises from the split between our higher self and our very human self. When our healthy ego experiences too much pain, when it is unable to digest the intensity of our experiences, it separates and goes adrift. Floating alone in the world with only part of what we need to live an integrated life, our ego convinces us to shun the other half of ourselves, ignoring the totality of who we are. Our ego splits off from our eternal essence, our true and authentic self. And then, in an attempt to make ourselves feel whole again, we create a false self, an outer wrapping, a veneer to cover up our now wounded inner world. It is then that the internal war begins.

What war? you might ask. The miserable war between the good self and the bad, the light and the dark, the id and the ego, the Jekyll and Hyde. The war is over territory, so-called land— meaning you. Which of these selves will conquer and gain free access to the human life that it embodies? Will it be the good sister or her evil twin, the inner force of divine good or the dark forces of the wounded self?

Once we understand the design of our humanity, we will know that we are both divine and human and that within each of us there is interplay of darkness and light, of good and bad. Our divine nature is known by many names: the holy self, the higher self, our spiritual core, the spirit, and the true self. The unhealthy or wounded ego is known as the shadow, the evil twin, the false self, or the lower self. In Eastern philosophy this duality is described as the yin and the yang, but these polarities have been referred to in countless ways: the Divine Self versus the Human Ego; the Collective Heart versus the Individual Mind; True Self versus False Self. Whatever terms you use, the point is that we have a higher self and a lower self, a finite self and an infinite self, and we need both in order to be whole. We are living an intricate human experience in which a state of harmony is naturally sought between these seemingly opposing aspects of ourselves whether we are conscious of it or not. But this balance cannot be achieved by simply trying to ignore our darker impulses; that leads only to greater separation and pain.

In psychological terms, this split is caused when we dissociate from and repress certain parts of ourselves. As the great Swiss psychologist Carl Jung was quoted as saying decades ago, "I'd rather be whole than good"; in other words, if we try to be only "good people" by splitting off or dissociating ourselves from the darker impulses that exist inside our ego structure, we cut ourselves off from the very essence of our humanity. And by repressing the dark side of ourselves, we are only inviting it to manifest itself in unhealthy ways. We have vivid examples of this phenomenon in the case of certain Catholic priests who deny their sexual needs and desires only to act them out by sexually assaulting innocent children. Or "the good girl" from a highly respected, philanthropic family who gets knocked up in the eighth grade by the town bad boy. Or the class valedictorian who gets caught cheating on his finals. We good people do bad things when we shun our basic human impulses and deny our pain, discontent, heartache, and conflicting urges. When out of shame we deny that we have human needs and human weaknesses, we blind ourselves to our essential nature and ignore the needs of our lower selves. Then, cut off from the purest part of ourselves, our source, we find ourselves vulnerable to expressing thoughts, behaviors, and urges that we never thought possible.

One of the most chilling stories depicting this core disconnection is Robert Louis Stevenson's *Strange Case of Dr. Jekyll and Mr. Hyde*. Although written as a horror mystery set in Victorian-era England, it is actually far more than a tale of the battle between morality and sin, between good and evil. Upon deeper examination, we find that it is a poignant allegory about the ravages of repression. Dr. Henry Jekyll is a respected physician and a gentleman, the epitome of virtue and goodness. But as a human being who possesses the full range of impulses, desires, needs, and capabilities, he secretly seeks freedom from the heavy burden of his own duality. Living inside a reality of utter control and total psychological constraint, Dr. Jekyll can explore his dark side only by drinking a magic potion that frees him from his inhibitions and allows his latent aspects to be expressed through his alter ego, the repulsive Edward Hyde.

Unable to summon the courage to recognize, acknowledge, and confront the dark side of himself, Dr. Jekyll then falls into the grips of substance addiction and becomes the prey of his own internal predator: the ravenous, insatiable desires and needs of his own rejected and abandoned self. Unable to constrain himself, Mr. Hyde preys on the weak—such as a feeble old man and an innocent little girl. Deeply afraid of losing his high status in society and feeling the shame of his humanity, this once kind and intelligent man becomes the victim of his own repressed nature. Unable or unwilling to meet his human needs with conscious awareness, and having no access to self-acceptance, humility, or remorse, Dr. Jekyll sees no alternatives to and no escape from what he imagines to be an irreconcilable split inside himself. Ultimately, he chooses death as a means to free both himself and Mr. Hyde.

The tale of Jekyll and Hyde is an extreme example, but the truth is that most of us serve two masters. Human consciousness is not "all of a piece," but is rather multiple, dynamic and inconsistent, volatile and fragile. As we work to maintain our daily awareness, paying attention to what is happening around us and inside us, our first master pushes us to maximize that awareness, to be a "good" human being who will succeed at the enterprise of life. Our second master, on the other hand, asks us to be a different kind of vessel: instead of being a container for greater awareness, we are asked to contain all of the conflicts, contradictions, ambiguities, ironies, paradoxes, and complexities of human life, which can erupt, often uninvited and in spite of our better wishes, corrupting our best intentions. This is the plight of our human experience.

Right now, within each of us there are two voices fighting to be heard: the voice of reason, good conscience, and the good of the greater whole; and the voice of fear, shame, and selfishness. The voice of our higher self versus the voice of our lower self. This is the dilemma, the inner struggle between the dark and the light aspects of our humanity. One voice is relaxed, trusting, and stable, while the other is fearful, nervous, and calculating. One holds the promise of serenity, peace of mind, and an innate knowledge that things are as they should be, while the other echoes the fragmented uncertainty of the unknown. One tells us to do the right thing, not to worry if our neighbors have more than us, and the other tells us to work harder, to find a way to get, collect, and win the prize for having the most toys. One tells us that we are in an abusive situation and should get out, while the other minimizes the destruction, saying, "You'll never find better than this." One says, "You are perfect as you are," while the other insists, "You're not pretty enough, smart enough, thin enough, or successful enough." One urges, "Get help, it's OK, we all have struggles to overcome," and the other taunts, teases, and humiliates us, constantly warning us that if we speak up about our dark thoughts, insecurities, and fears, we will be shunned, punished, or abandoned.

These two opposing forces are part of our human hard wiring. There is absolutely nothing we can do to eliminate either one of them, nor would we want to. When we understand them both and allow them to operate in the manner in which they were designed, we find ourselves eternally grateful that we possess both of these forces. We can work to suppress them, hide them, deny them, ignore them, and mute them, but they will always be there whether we want to acknowledge them or not. They will be there in times of inner peace and in times of conflict. Although these voices sound a bit different within each of us, their agendas are the same. One voice is there to lift us out of the smallness of our individual dramas, and the other is there to keep us deeply embedded in the familiar ground of our lowest self. One strives to support us in evolving our souls and embracing the larger whole, and the other tries to keep us firmly rooted in our own individual needs and perspectives. One works to ensure that our lives matter and that we make a difference in the world, while the other will constantly tempt us, steering us away from our commitments and our integrity. One will urge us to do the right thing as the other leads us right into temptation.

One voice will tell us to indulge in a nice piece of chocolate cake, while the other lets us know that the bite of cake will kill our diet and leave us feeling bad about ourselves for days. One will see something it wants and try to figure out a way to get it, while the other will warn us that it's wrong to steal. One will tell us to eat and purge, while the other will firmly let us know that we are sick and need help. One will shout out for another round, one more drink, while the other says we've had enough.

One will want to buy that beautiful pair of shoes or go away for that luxurious weekend jaunt, while the other will remind us that we've gone way over our budget and are deeply in debt. One will tell us to skip paying our taxes, while the other reminds us that to do so is against the law.

One will lie without a second thought, while the other will make us aware of the deceit. One will say, "Cheating isn't right," while the other will lust out loud, egging us on in the violation. One will say, "But look at all the good things I do. It doesn't matter if a few people get hurt along the way," while the other will say, "Stop. You're hurting other people." One will let us know when enough is enough, while the other pleads, "If I stop, I'll die." One will say, "You must be right at any cost," while the other gently lets us know that to be human is to err and sometimes we make mistakes. One will lash out at our children in rage and frustration, and the other will remind us that they are precious souls who deserve our love and patience. One drives us to move so fast that we don't have time to think things through, while the other says, "Stop, take a breath, and consider the consequences of your behavior."

This is an age-old struggle between the two opposing forces that lie within each of us, each force fighting for survival while at the same time trying to come to terms with the other: the divine force that expands and uplifts us, that inspires us to share our unique gifts for the benefit of the world; and the force that holds us back, that traps us in the smallness of our lowest thoughts and feeds on our most primal and selfish urges.

These two forces wage an internal war, and the battleground is our consciousness. The force that wins has the ability to bring us joy, success, love, and a sense of belonging, or to rob us of opportunities and bring us unhappiness, misery, and suffering. These two forces with two seemingly opposing agendas struggle to dominate our life. Which one will win?

Many Selves, One Master

There is an old Cherokee story about a chief of a large village. One day the chief decides that the time has come to teach his favorite grandson about life. He takes him out into the forest, sits him under an old tree, and explains, "Son, there is a fight going on within the mind and heart of every human being that is alive today. Even though I am a wise old chief, the leader of our people, this same fight is going on inside me. If you do not know that the battle is going on, it will drive you crazy. You will never know what direction to go in. You will sometimes win in life, and then, without understanding why, you will suddenly find yourself lost, confused, and afraid, and may lose all that you worked so hard to gain. You will often think you are doing the right thing and then find out that you were making the wrong choices. If you do not understand the forces of good and evil, the individual life and the collective life, the true self and the false self, you will live a life always in great turmoil.

"It is as if there are two big wolves living inside me; one is white and one is black. The white wolf is good, kind, and does no harm. He lives in harmony with all that is around him and does not take offense when no offense was intended. The good wolf, grounded and strong in the understanding of who he is and what he is capable of, fights only when it is right to do so and when he must in order to protect himself or his family, and even then he does it in the right way. He looks out for all the other wolves in his pack and never deviates from his nature.

"But there is a black wolf also that lives inside me, and this wolf is very different. He is loud, angry, discontent, jealous, and afraid. The littlest thing will set him off into a fit of rage. He fights with everyone, all the time, for no reason. He cannot think clearly because his greed for more and his anger and hate are so great. But it is helpless anger, son, for his anger will change nothing. He looks for trouble wherever he goes, so he easily finds it. He trusts no one, so he has no real friends."

The old chief sits in silence for a few minutes, letting the story of the two wolves penetrate his young grandson's mind. Then he slowly bends down, looks deeply into his grandson's eyes, and confesses, "Sometimes it's hard to live with these two wolves inside me, for both of them fight hard to dominate my spirit."

Riveted by his elder's account of this great internal battle, the boy tugs on his grandfather's breechcloth and anxiously asks, "Which one of the wolves wins, Grandfather?" And with a knowing smile and a strong, firm voice, the chief says, "They both do, son. You see, if I choose to feed only the white wolf, the black wolf will be waiting around every corner looking to see when I am off balance or too busy to pay attention to one of my responsibilities, and he will attack the white wolf and cause many problems for me and our tribe. He will always be angry and fighting to get the attention he craves. But if I pay a little attention to the black wolf because I understand his nature, if I acknowledge him for the strong force that he is and let him know that I respect him for his character and will use him to help me if we as a tribe are ever in big trouble, he will be happy, the white wolf will be happy, and they both win. We all win."

Confused, the boy asks, "I don't understand, Grandfather. How can both wolves win?" The chief continues: "You see, son, the black wolf has many important qualities that I might need, depending on what comes our way. He is fierce, strong-willed, and will not back down for a moment. He is smart, clever, and is capable of the most devious thoughts and strategies, which are important in a time of war. He has many sharp and heightened senses that only one who is looking through the eyes of darkness could appreciate. In the midst of an attack he could be our greatest ally." The chief then brings out some cold steaks from his pouch and puts them down on the ground, one to his left and one to his right. He points to the steaks and says, "Over here to my left is food for the white wolf, and here to my right is food for the black wolf. If I choose to feed them both, they will no longer fight to get my attention, and I can use each of them as needed. And since there is no war going on between the two of them, I can hear the voice of my deeper knowing and choose which one can help me best in every circumstance. If your grandmother wants food to cook for a special meal and I haven't taken care of it like I should have, I can ask the white wolf to lend me his charms to console her black wolf, who is hungry and angry. The white wolf always knows what to say and will help me be more sensitive to her needs. You see, son, if you understand that there are two main forces that exist inside you and you give them both equal respect, they will both win and there will be peace. Peace, my son, is the Cherokee mission— the ultimate purpose of life. A man who has peace inside has everything. A man who is pulled apart by the war inside him has nothing. You are a young man who has to choose how you will interact with the opposing forces that live inside you. What you decide will determine the quality of the rest of your life. And when one of the wolves needs special attention, which it will sometimes, you don't have to be ashamed; you can just admit it to your elders and get the help you need. When it is out in the open, others who have struggled with this same battle can offer you their wisdom."

This simple and poignant story explains the plight of the human experience. Each of us is engaged in a continual struggle as the forces of lightness and darkness battle for our attention and our allegiance. Both the light and the dark reside inside us at the same time. Truth be told, there is a whole pack of wolves running around inside us—the loving wolf, the kindhearted wolf, the smart wolf, the sensitive wolf, the strong wolf, the selfless wolf, the openhearted wolf, and the creative wolf. Along with these positive aspects exist the dissatisfied wolf, the ungrateful wolf, the entitled wolf, the nasty wolf, the selfish wolf, the shameful wolf, the lying wolf, and the destructive wolf. Each day we have the opportunity to acknowledge all of these wolves, all these parts of ourselves, and we get to choose how we will relate to each of them. Will we stand in judgment on some and pretend some don't exist, or are we going to take ownership of the entire pack?

Why is it that we feel the need to deny the pack of wolves that lives within us? The answer is easy. We either think they don't exist or think they shouldn't exist. We fear that if we admit to all the different selves that occupy space in our psyche, we will somehow be labeled as weird, different, damaged, or psychologically fragmented. We think we should be "normal" good people who have only one person dwelling inside them. But there are many selves, and the refusal to come to terms with them is a grave error—one that will lead us to commit stupid and reckless acts of self-sabotage.

Here is the big secret: there are many selves contained within our "self," because within each of us exists every possible quality. There is nothing that we can see, and nothing that we can judge, that we are not. We are all the light and the dark, the saint and the sinner, the lovable and the unlovable. We are all kind and warm as well as coldhearted and mean. Within you and within me lies every quality known to humankind. Although we may not be consciously aware of all of the qualities we possess, they are lying dormant within us and can come forth at any time, anywhere. Understanding this allows us to comprehend why all of us "good people" are capable of doing such bad things and, more important, why at times we become our own worst enemies.

3

THE SEESAW

In his book *In Search of the Miraculous*, P. D. Ouspensky, a student of the Russian spiritual teacher G. I. Gurdjieff, told a story that captures the multiplicity of human awareness. "It is the greatest mistake," he said, "to think that man is always one and the same. A man is never the same for long. He is continually changing. He seldom remains the same even for half an hour. We think that if a man is called Ivan he is always Ivan. Nothing of the kind. Now he is Ivan, in another minute he is Peter, and a minute later he is Nicholas, Sergius, Matthew, Simon. And all of you think he is Ivan. You know that Ivan cannot do a certain thing. He cannot tell a lie for instance. Then you find out he has told a lie and you are surprised he could have done so. And, indeed, Ivan cannot lie; it is Nicholas who lied. And when the opportunity presents itself Nicholas cannot help lying. You will be astonished when you realize what a multitude of these Ivans and Nicholases live in one man."

Every one of us is capable of humility and arrogance, generosity and greed, peacefulness and violence. You can think of each of these pairs of opposites as resting on one end of a seesaw. When we own and embrace each of the extremes, the seesaw is balanced. But when we suppress one extreme in an attempt to show the world only the bright side of our persona, when we try to manage our dark tendencies rather than make peace with them, we go dangerously out of balance. And because our psyches are always seeking wholeness and balance, it is only a matter of time before our dark side rears its ugly head, threatening to undermine and destroy all that we stand for.

All of us have all these qualities hardwired into us. Within our DNA we hold the potential of every quality that we can see in another. The human condition is one of polarities. It is a paradox. Being blind to this paradox and in denial of our whole or true self—especially being in denial of traits that are the *polar opposites* of what we wish to be true about ourselves—is what causes us untold pain and suffering and greatly increases the likelihood that we will sabotage our lives.

The denial of the totality of our humanity limits what we are able to see about ourselves and others and cuts us off from the very resource we need in order to live fulfilled, happy, and successful lives. *What is this resource?* you might ask. It's simple: the resource is truth. When we are willing to embrace the human paradox, we become conscious and aware enough to be truthful with ourselves. Only then can we finally see with clear and honest eyes who we are and what we are capable of. Truth is the essential ingredient we each need to ensure that our "whole self," and not our "evil twin," is the one who is making the decisions about our behavior and directing our choices.

If we surmise that good people can't do bad things, we have to ask ourselves who is the one actually doing the bad thing. Is the good person really bad? After all, what is a good person? Are we only good or bad—no gray or chartreuse, just black and white? If "good" people cannot do bad things, then who within us commits such acts? Most of us just think of ourselves one-sidedly as good and don't engage the shadow of that one-sided thinking. This is a narrow perspective on our humanity that leads us to distorted and righteous beliefs that dangerously limit the way we view ourselves, others, and the world.

There is a moral effort required to understand that we are all capable of the most heinous acts and self-destructive behaviors. Psychological laziness characterizes most of our adaptation to life, where the good resides within us and the bad gets projected onto others. Such is the case of the high-ranking, outspoken political officer pointing his finger at the president for having an affair—standing before reporters and millions of Americans expressing his outrage at the president's impeachable offense—and then later being discovered as having had an extramarital affair of his own at the same time.

And then we have the senior pastor of a fourteen-thousand-member church who self-righteously condemns homosexuality and holds a firm stand against gay marriage but then is forced to resign from his position following the public announcement by a gay prostitute that he had had a three-year relationship with the pastor.

Or the former Senate majority leader whose private segregationist views popped up at a very public hundredth-birthday celebration for Strom Thurmond, sending shock waves through the country. In a December 2002 article, journalist Bob Weir insightfully described this verbal disaster, this unconscious act of self-sabotage, as "an involuntary eruption of primal prejudices that have been held captive by the constraints of propriety." I couldn't have said it better.

Our disowned, rejected selves and the shame they hold provide the secret answer to the question of why we are our own worst enemy. But if it's true that we are not as good as we think we are, if there is more to us than we let on, even to ourselves, what are we to do about it?

Tending to Your Inner World

Even though we may watch in disbelief as other people commit crimes of passion, stupidity, or greed, and scream, "I could never do that!", studies have shown that, given the right or wrong set of circumstances, most of us can be swayed, thrown off course, and convinced to participate in behaviors that we would never believe ourselves capable of. Most of us can and will display behaviors and qualities in our lifetimes that we never imagined ourselves capable of—abandoning our partners, taking what isn't ours, positioning ourselves advantageously at the expense of another, or lying to cover a misdeed or bad habit.

There are many disowned aspects of ourselves that can and will act out autonomously, whether we want to believe it or not. They live in the dark recesses of our wounded egos. Our shadows can be thought of as a collection of these partial selves, existing just beneath the surface of our awareness. When ignored, they become powerful forces that can act as independent entities. They can pop up at any time in our lives, robbing us of the very things we have worked so hard to achieve. They can sabotage our relationships, our finances, our families, and our futures, and yet most of us choose to deny their very existence. We work diligently to ignore these aspects of ourselves. We unknowingly use food, alcohol, sex, drugs, excitement, collecting, gossiping, and philandering as ways to distract ourselves from seeing that which we deem unacceptable or unflattering.

We do bad things to others and ourselves when we cannot or will not admit that there is more to us than we can see or know. But we must understand that each part of ourselves has an essential need that requires our attention, and when we choose to consistently ignore the needs of our many selves we are in danger of losing control of our behavior and becoming our own worst enemies. Our shame over these rejected parts and their unmet needs drives us to shut off our deeper knowing of right and wrong and what is ultimately in our highest and best interest.

When we understand that we are all simultaneously "good" people and "bad" people, we are better able to withhold our judgments and stop pointing our fingers at those who get caught acting out their darker impulses. We will see them for what they are—the poor souls who got caught with their pants down when their dark side took over; when some quality they thought they had successfully suppressed sprang to life. Or when a wound so deep and so painful became exposed that they reacted without thinking, without even considering the consequences of their behavior. When we understand who we are at the deepest level, how we are designed, and what drives us to do what we do, we will see just how predictable the human experience can be. We'll see the hidden reasons we do the things we do, react the way we do—even when we consciously don't want to. We'll come face-to-face with the reality that more often than not we are puppets, slaves to the internal programming that drives our actions, our reactions, our choices, and, ultimately, our behaviors.

4

SHAME ON YOU

Unacknowledged and unprocessed shame is what causes us to sabotage our own success, violate our own self-interest, take what isn't ours, get swept away by our old addictions, and destroy our relationships. Self-sabotage is our way of externalizing our internal shame—meaning, we unconsciously do something to shame ourselves so that we can heal the incident that caused us to feel the shame in the first place. Another way to say this is: if we don't deal with our shame, it will deal with us. If we continue to ignore or repress our shame, we will express it in some self-destructive way. This is why it is vital that we deal with the pain of our past, learn from it, and use it to grow and to contribute to the greater whole; then, we don't have to do something to externalize that which we cannot see. When we understand shame's intrinsic value, we will see it for what it is—a spiritual guide to help us understand and know ourselves at the deepest level, heal our emotional wounds, and deactivate our negative programming. It's a spiritual treatment—our soul's way of guiding us back home to our authentic nature.

Acts of self-sabotage may seem to come out of the blue, but I would argue that they are nature's way of showing us our hidden internal shame and the split inside ourselves. We might succeed at keeping our shame hidden for a while—until one day just the right set of circumstances comes along to remind us of that which we have buried deep inside. Maybe feelings of failure, incompetence, and unworthiness begin to rattle our internal world, making us anxious, bitter, and self-doubting. Or maybe our shame gets triggered as we realize that others have achieved a level of fulfillment beyond our own. It may happen when we reach a level of success, affluence, love, or admiration that is outside our familiar comfort zone. Fearing that we will no longer belong or that people will be jealous of us, or feeling ashamed that we are more gifted or talented than our siblings or friends, we put on the self-imposed brakes. In other words, we sabotage the success that could be ours.

Some people use their fall from the top as evidence that they are weak and flawed, or just as mediocre as the rest of us. This was the case for William W., an eighteen-year-old star baseball player who had just received a contract for over $3 million to play for a major-league team. Less than two weeks later, he got drunk, picked a fight, got arrested, and in that one act lost his contract and threw away his dreams. Or take the case of the young starlet who goes from being in the limelight to repeatedly getting arrested for driving under the influence of alcohol and drugs. With a few bad choices she manages to expose her deep pain and shame, proving that she is no more worthy of adoration than the rest of us. No matter what the act of self-sabotage is—

no matter how far the fall from the top or how big the climb out of the gutter—if the pain is severe enough, we become open to glimpsing the self that exists outside our ego structure. Pain and shame remain the most dramatic catalysts for evoking change in a human being. But to deal with our internal shame we must first understand what it is and where it comes from.

If you have the courage to examine the mechanics of being human, you will soon realize that you possess a wider range of human qualities than you imagine, a wider range of human behaviors than you care to acknowledge. But the question arises: why do you shun the whole of who you are? The answer is simple: because you were trained as a young child to *not* be yourself. You were conditioned to believe that if you came forward as your whole, authentic self, expressing all parts of yourself (both light and dark, good and bad), you would be shunned, rejected, and labeled. So before you could even write a sentence, you began the painful and sorrowful process of separating from the totality of your whole being, all in the name of wanting to be loved, to be accepted, and to belong.

This is how it works: One day, I come home from work and ask my warm and loving three-year-old son, "Beau, did you get your hair washed?" And without a flinch he answers, "Yes, Mommy." I am relieved. As the nanny is saying good-bye and walking out the door, she turns to me and says, "Oh, and he wouldn't let me wash his hair." So here I am, standing next to what is the most precious thing in the world to me and realizing he is a . . . yes, you got it . . . a liar. I'm mortified. How could it be, my beautiful boy lying to me? A few days go by, I ask some friends over and bring out a plate of four cookies, and I ask Beau, "How many cookies do you want?" And he replies, "Four," so I know he's . . . that's right . . . greedy.

A few weeks later, after having been in the park with him for hours one day, we return home and I go into my office to get some work done. Beau comes in, and I ask him, "Is it Beau time, or is it Mommy time?" And with a warmhearted smile he innocently blurts out, "It's Beau time!" So I know he is . . . selfish. So here I am with a loving, kind, warm, sweet three-year-old whom I love more than anything in the world, and he has already shown signs of being a lying, greedy, selfish human. And I know that if I'm to be a good mother, what I'm supposed to teach him is that it's not OK to be *that*. If I am good I will tell him, "Don't be selfish, Beau. Nobody likes selfish people"; "Don't lie, Beau, or I'll punish you and withhold my love"; "Don't be greedy, Beau, or you won't have any friends." I am supposed to shame him and punish him so that he hides these impulses and behaviors. I am supposed to teach him that good people don't do these things. But he already has shown these qualities. He's already lied, been selfish, and been greedy. He's already taken a toy out of the hands of a little girl and shoved another toddler while racing to the pony ride. And again, if I'm to be a good mother, I'm supposed to tell him, "Don't be that; don't do that!" I am torn, because I know that if I shame him he will internalize one message, a message I have seen thousands of people struggle with, a message I know most men and women have: There is something wrong with me. I'm not OK. I'm not worthy. I am bad.

I struggled in the knowledge that if he naturally showed his human impulses and I shamed him for them, he would wind up with the same shame-filled internal programming as the rest of us. I was horrified by this thought as I became present to why we reject, suppress, hate, and are embarrassed by parts of our humanity. Beau is no different from every other kid in his age range.

He's a normal, healthy child with normal human impulses. But he is human—perfect and imperfect, just like you and me.

I wanted to find a way to teach Beau that there may be a time when a dose of greed would help him to save money for his future, or when his selfishness would allow him to set a strong boundary with a schoolmate or a co-worker. I wanted him to know that if an Internet predator asked for his name, it would be acceptable to lie and fabricate a fake identity—maybe even embellishing the lie by telling the would-be perpetrator not that he is fourteen years old and home alone, but rather that he is a forty-five-year-old law enforcement officer who knows who he is and where he is.

As a mother, I want my son to understand that there is light and dark, good and bad, and a curse as well as a blessing, in every aspect of our humanity. And I have found no greater story than one I heard from Guru Mayi, the leader of the Siddha Yoga Foundation, to illustrate this point.

One day, the ruler of a prosperous kingdom sends for one of his messengers. When he arrives the king tells him to go out and find the worst thing in the entire world, and bring it back within a few days. The messenger departs, and returns days later, empty-handed. Puzzled, the king asks, "What have you discovered? I don't see anything." The messenger says, "Right here, Your Majesty," and sticks out his tongue. Bewildered, the king asks the young man to explain. The messenger says, "My tongue is the worst thing in the world. My tongue can do many horrible things. My tongue speaks evil and tells lies. I can overindulge with my tongue, which leaves me feeling tired and sick, and I can say things that hurt other people. My tongue is the worst thing in the world." Pleased, the king then commands the messenger to go out and find him the best thing in the entire world.

The messenger leaves hurriedly, and once again he comes back days later with nothing in his hands. "Where is it?" the king shouts out. Again, the messenger sticks out his tongue. "How can this be?" the kings asks. "Explain it to me." The messenger replies, "My tongue is the best thing in the world. My tongue is a messenger of love. Only with my tongue can I express the overwhelming beauty of poetry. My tongue teaches me refinement in tastes and guides me to choose foods that will nourish my body. My tongue is the best thing in the entire world because it allows me to chant the name of God."

From the beginning of our lives we are trained to reject and suppress certain parts of who we are because we believe they are bad. But the moment we close the door on one of these aspects of ourselves, we set in motion the battle with our dark side. Denial of self, whether through repression, suppression, or rejection, is the food that sustains and nourishes our dark impulses, which lead us to spontaneous acts of self-sabotage. We are told, "Don't be angry, don't be selfish, and don't be greedy!" *Don't be* is the message that is ingrained in us early on in life, and once we have determined, out of fear and shame, the multitude of qualities that we must reject, this internal message drives our every behavior and choice.

Whether we're aware of it or not, we are all running from the devastating feelings of shame, humiliation, and embarrassment. We go to great lengths to avoid feeling the raw pain that comes from our perception that we're not good enough. We work hard to conceal the fact that we believe we're on the outside, separate and alone due to our own perceived flaws and failings as a human being. We try desperately to keep from feeling this shame, which hangs like a two-ton anchor around our necks, killing off our dreams, our passion, and our joy.

In order to break free of what theologian and psychologist John Bradshaw refers to as the shame that binds us, we need to distinguish healthy shame from toxic shame. Healthy shame is a built-in mechanism that is designed to support us in recognizing when we are behaving in acceptable ways and when we are not. This healthy feeling of shame is like an internal barometer that lets us know when we are operating inside our integrity and when we have deviated from it. It acts as an alarm that alerts us when we have strayed away from our highest or true self and are making choices from our lower self. Healthy shame produces feelings and sensations inside our bodies that help us to recognize when we have gone off course. Like an internal compass, healthy shame tries its best to guide us and keep us moving toward our highest potential, whatever that might be. It is instinctual, natural, and needed if we are to monitor our behavior. Healthy shame is built into our human operating system. We've all experienced the feeling in our body that lets us know we are doing something—or are about to do something—that is inappropriate. For example, if we drink to the point where we begin slurring our words at the dinner table, healthy shame lets us know we are embarrassing ourselves. If we're standing too close to a friend's husband or wearing something that is too revealing, the voice of healthy shame tells us to back up or cover ourselves. We are all born with this mechanism, and when we tune in to it and can distinguish it, it acts as a great supporter and friend.

On the other hand, toxic shame is the result of our programming. It enters our system as a negative message we internalize from someone else or as a lie we tell ourselves. Then, like mold, our toxic shame grows in the dark, hidden recesses of our inner world. It becomes thick and dense, covering us like a thick film, eroding our self-esteem and suffocating our sense of self-worth. Each incident that made us feel ugly, less than, stupid, or unworthy added to the growth of this toxic shame, making it harder and harder for us to recognize our authentic self. As we internalized more and more shame-based messages, we unconsciously began to create what I call a *shame body*. Stored within our shame body is the sum of all the negative messages we received from those around us. And whether these messages were sent intentionally or unconsciously, they produced the same result. Within our shame body exist thousands of tiny wounds that all have loud voices telling us to "watch out" and "be careful" because at any time those giant judges—the big creatures we called adults, parents, teachers, and priests—will come out against us with their swords, otherwise known as their judgments. Or perhaps parents or caregivers unknowingly or knowingly chiseled away at our most precious gift, the only one we knew—the authentic and free expression of ourselves. They ridiculed us for laughing too loudly, for playing too much, for not wanting to eat all the vegetables on our plate. They teased us when we were needy and made fun of us when we were "scaredy-cats." They pointed their fingers at us when we did something stupid, and they hollered at us when we were about to touch something that was theirs. They angrily reprimanded us or pulled our arms when we were lagging behind. They got on our backs when we were happy and when we were sad, when we asked for too much, or when we sulked in our rooms because we were deemed spoiled rotten and selfish.

Since we were no longer able to love ourselves as we were—since we feared that our true self was really unlovable, faulty, worthless, and unacceptable—we unconsciously made the devastating decision that we were bad and undeserving of love, care, respect, and success. All these thoughts and fears led us to create the negative beliefs that are our deepest source of shame: *Who I am is not OK. I am bad.*

For most of us, the voice of "You are bad" was everywhere when we were growing up—sometimes subtle, sometimes not so subtle; sometimes loud, sometimes a soft whisper. But no matter what the tone, these messages of shame all had the same deadening, toxic effect. They all instilled fear in us, giving birth to our shame body. Our shame body is an unconscious state of being, an invisible capsule surrounding us, that is stuffed with every negative message that we couldn't understand or was too painful to deal with. These shame-filled messages, whether delivered silently or out loud, caused us to internalize—to embody—some version of this message: *"There is something wrong with me.* I'm not a good boy or girl. . . . I'm going to get in trouble; I deserve to be punished. I deserve to go without. . . . I deserve it because I am *bad."* Then, unknowingly, we made the commitment that if someone else wasn't battering or emotionally torturing us, we would torture ourselves with our own acts of self-sabotage, because we believed that bad people deserve to have bad things happen to them. We believed that bad people don't deserve love and happiness. Think about this: If, deep inside, you have been programmed with toxic, self-deprecating messages like these, what else would you expect to unconsciously attract into your life? And what's most frightening is that because we have been trained to focus on the outer world—on securing love, money, success, fun, sex, or our next meal—most of us remain unaware that these messages are alive and well, running, day in and day out, in the background of our subconscious minds.

You Are Bad

Imagine this for a moment. The message of "You are bad" was taught to you, mirrored to you (i.e., you saw it being done to others around you), and imprinted on you tens of thousands of times before you were even ten years old. Even if you were one of the lucky few who were told constantly how great you were, you still got the message if you happened to display the opposite behavior of the one being praised. If you are human, it's inevitable that you imprinted some version of these shameful messages. The admonishments were everywhere. Often without malice we were told:

"Bad girl! Why did you wet your bed again?"

"Good girls don't talk like that."

"Good boys don't lie."

"Good girls don't talk that loudly."

"Good boys don't interrupt."

"Good children should be seen and not heard."

"Only good girls and boys get to do special things."

"Bad boy! I'm taking away your teddy bear right now if you don't clean up your mess."

"I don't want to hear your whiny voice."

"Don't be a sissy."

"I can't take you anymore. Get away from me!"

Many of these messages were, of course, intended to help us fit in, get along, and grow up to be good and proper ladies and gentlemen. Nevertheless, the message "You are bad" came through loud and clear.

If I spent a few days with you, I could fill an encyclopedia-sized book with all the bad things that were said and done to you—and show you how these negative emotions have become ingrained in your subconscious and are directing your choices and behaviors. Most of the people I have met in my life—with good parents and bad—have had this message told to them in one way or another, thousands and thousands of times. Whether you realize it or not, you internalized these thoughts and feelings over and over, and because of this, these negative, often poisonous messages now live inside you.

This process didn't happen consciously. It didn't happen because you weighed the facts, thought through the opinions and behaviors of those around you, or analyzed the validity of the messages you heard. In fact, most of what occurred and shaped your life happened at a time before you had access to intellectual reasoning skills—before you could even consciously judge or assess those who were delivering these messages. Still, you unknowingly assigned meaning to their words, made decisions based on their actions, and allowed negative interpretations to be etched into your psyche (your human software). You participated in the building of your shame body without even knowing it was happening.

Toxic shame is at the root of why we do bad things and why bad things happen to us. It begins when we unknowingly internalize the shame of not being good enough. We internalize this shame without realizing how susceptible our precious young psyches are. Even if we had the best parents in the world, every time we displayed one of our less attractive human behaviors, every time we did not meet their standards or did something that could be considered socially unacceptable, the "You are bad" message was delivered, and we internalized it.

Private Acts of Shame

None of us goes unscathed when it comes to shame. Maybe it began in the privacy of your bedroom. Maybe you had a sister who rubbed up against you or lured you into playing doctor, or a father who visited you in the middle of the night, planning to take inappropriate sexual liberties. Maybe it was a babysitter, a family friend, or a mother who held you too close or an uncle who ran his hands over you in a way that violated your healthy boundaries. Maybe you were warned about being sexual with someone in the family yet it seemed natural in the moment to be kissing cousins, and so you did. Maybe you were the one who convinced your young sister to take off her underpants or show her private parts to your friends. Or maybe, in a quest to satisfy a healthy sexual desire, you took the end of your hairbrush and stuck it inside you, or put your private parts in a place they didn't belong. In the end, your curiosity and sexual desire may have been met, but your shame may have overridden the few minutes of pleasure that you received, leaving an indelible mark on your memory, your psyche, and your self-image.

Shame-filled and shameful sexual behaviors happen every day in every kind of family, every class, every culture, and every economic bracket. They usually happen without either party thinking about the consequences of their actions. There is usually one perpetrator and one victim. One person may be haunted by the act for years, while another tries to pass it off as if it were no big deal. But whether you are aware of it or not, if you have a conscience you will store this private act of shame in your subconscious, and you will more than likely use it against yourself in the future.

Stacey J. was raised in an emotionally chaotic environment where she lived full-time with her loving but alcoholic mother and rage-prone stepfather and spent weekends with her passive, G-rated father and devout Methodist grandmother. As an eight-year-old girl, she frequently overheard her mother and stepfather having sex and received a wrenching double hit of shame—that she even heard them in the first place, and that she was actually aroused by their sounds of pleasure. Inside her unformed psyche, it was all very wrong: you're not supposed to see or hear your parents' sexual acts, and you're especially not supposed to be turned on by them!

Her shame was compounded by her snooping around and excavating hidden issues of *Playboy, Hustler,* and other porn magazines, finding nude Polaroid shots of her parents, being sexually fondled by a neighbor and French-kissed by an "uncle." With increasing incidents of sexually "bad" thoughts, behaviors, and experiences, this nice, quiet, agreeable, placating little midwestern girl was simmering with shame that would have to spill over at some point.

One of those moments arrived on an overcast Sunday morning when Stacey was eight years old. She had spent the weekend at her grandmother's house and somehow, miraculously, got out of going to church that morning. Out of the blue—and inside a very rare moment of being alone in a house without the constraints of adult eyes—she found herself spontaneously and intensely excited by the idea of exposing her naked butt in her grandmother's living-room picture window. So on this day— God's day—in a neighborhood that was typically abuzz with fathers mowing lawns, mothers gardening, and children playing, Stacey felt the wild rush of slowly pulling her pants down and rubbing her rear end against the large pane of glass. After a few minutes of this, her naughty euphoria turned into one of the defining moments of her childhood: her grandmother, sister, father, and his girlfriend returned from church, pulling up to the curb directly in front of the picture window. The first person to see her naked ass was, of course, her Jesus-loving grandmother.

What happened immediately after this incident (hiding behind a door, getting her father's belt across her bare behind, spending the rest of that painfully long day banished to the guest room, and having the story relayed to her mother, who could determine further punishment) was nothing compared with the depths of private shame she plunged herself into. From that day on, the belief that she was abnormal, deviant, twisted, and irreparably flawed became an integral part of the story of who she was. When she was only eight years old, Stacey's sexual shame became a bottom-line issue that would end up shaping her life.

After an adolescence of being sexually abused by a family member and a young adulthood that included countless sexual partners (usually while under the influence of alcohol and drugs) and three abortions, she grew up to be a woman who is seventy pounds overweight, chronically single, and aching for the return of her sexual self—all conditions about which she is deeply ashamed.

Public Displays of Shame

We see evidence of shame all around us. Examples are splashed across our magazine covers and TV screens. In our twenty-four-hour-a-day news and tabloid culture, public acts of shame have become commonplace.

We need go no further than our television sets, car radios, or the checkout lane at the grocery store to see shame on parade—to witness the distorted spectacle of ourselves, a ludicrous exaggeration of what it looks like to fall down and be humiliated in public. Courtroom TV, reality shows (especially those based on competition and getting "voted off"), tabloid TV shows, shock jock talk radio, and gossip rags all feed us sensationalistic stories that usually have absolutely no relevance to our day-to-day lives. But they do give us an unconscious outlet for playing out the ravaging criticism and judgments we have about our own humanity. With a foul-smelling mix of condescension, contempt, ridicule, and pity, we get to say things like "What was he thinking?! Spoiled brat! Serves her right! How stupid could he be?! Poor thing, all that money and she's just so out of touch with reality." We get to think to ourselves, "Sure, I may have some issues, but at least I'm not *that* bad!" We're voyeurs who get some relief from our own emotional pain by watching the blunders of those who have had the "audacity" to step out into the public eye and the downfalls of those who have stumbled into the limelight. And in a media-driven consumer culture that would hardly exist without shame and humiliation, the old advertising adage "Sex sells" could easily be replaced with "Shame sells." And it's no surprise that shame sells, since all of us were programmed with it and those messages became a part of our human software.

The Virus in Your Software

Our human software runs in the forefront of our minds, telling us where we can go, with whom we can go, and what is possible for us when we get there. Most of us will never know ourselves outside the confines of this automatic conditioning. We will never know what's possible beyond our current belief systems constructed by our shame and fear. These messages are deeply encoded in our psyches. They might take different forms, they might sound a bit different for each of us, but the messages are there. They are part of how we get socialized. If we didn't have these messages, how would we know how to behave? Can you begin to grasp the implications of these sabotage-producing messages that we all received? Here it is again: We are all deeply wounded by our society's socialization techniques. We are inadvertently taught that if we don't act in particular ways, it must mean that we are bad or no good. Even though we are unaware of and can't see this inner software, it is ingrained and encoded with the messaging we received, and it's always running in the background, fueling our self-doubt and our fears.

We are designed to attract to ourselves what is in alignment with what we believe to be true about ourselves and to push away what is not, and we are masters at doing it. Every belief holds a specific resonance, a vibration—and, as the saying goes, like attracts like. When we are young, we believe that the whole world is open to us and that we can do and be everything that we desire. If we fall we can usually get right back up. We are driven by the naïveté of our youth and are being pulled fearlessly ahead by our deepest hopes and desires. The power of our youth holds so much promise and potential that we unknowingly override the subconscious beliefs that have been programmed into us. We haven't yet fully bought into the belief that life might fail us or that bad things may happen to us that will prevent us from getting where we want to go. I would say we are still building our personas. But as that power becomes overridden by years of disappointment and pain, we no longer have the resources available to us that we did when we were young. At some point we stop living inside the endless possibilities of our youth and come face-to-face with our internal programming—our limited, self-shaming, often self-sabotaging, disconnected self. We leave the innocence of youth behind us and kick into the next stage of our lives, one that demands that we begin to learn from our past, examine our behaviors, and dissect our patterns so that we might become fully functioning, healthy, thriving human beings.

Your shame may have you believe that you are bad to the bone, rotten, worthless, stupid, good for nothing, foolish, mean, inconsiderate, weak, out of control, a liar, or any number of things. And then you unconsciously are drawn to exactly those people, circumstances, and behaviors that will reflect back to you your learned beliefs about yourself. Then, once you have participated unknowingly in creating outer circumstances that confirm your innermost beliefs, you seal the deal by acting out and proving that indeed you really are the bad one. Without any clue as to what you are doing, you verify the very belief about yourself that caused you the most shame and suffering.

Since we are always attracting what we are most committed to, especially the underlying commitments of our subconscious mind, we create and attract situations in our lives that reflect back to us our internal beliefs, even the damaging ones loaded with shame. Then, our outer circumstances—oftentimes precipitated by our own behavior—prove to us in various ways that we really *aren't* good enough, that we *are* bad boys and girls, that we *don't* deserve happiness, health, joy, and abundance. Thus, we solidify and perpetuate the very lies we bought into decades ago.

Because we are spiritual beings who can see our inner programming only by looking into the outside world, we unconsciously draw forth in the outer world circumstances to externalize our inner shame; hence the birth of our own self-sabotage and the excruciating and repetitive cycles of victimhood and self-destruction. If we want to understand why good people do bad things and why we become our own worst enemies, we must be willing to acknowledge the devastating effects of our internal programming.

This programming acts like an insidious computer virus that can wipe out all the good in our lives. And as long as these messages are silently running in the background, like a virus in our subconscious minds, we will continue to send forth into the outer world the low resonance of this corrupted message. We will continue to act out or unknowingly attract to us the outer expression of our internal beliefs. Even though they may be deeply hidden, disguised, and suppressed so that our conscious minds are unaware they even exist, they transmit a powerful force that drives us to act in ways that will bring situations into our lives that seem to justify our deeply ingrained shame. The mechanism of our humanity acts like a projector. When I believe I'm a failure, I create and attract experiences that are in complete alignment with this belief. Then one day I wake up inside that reality, and I'm shocked by what is going on in my life. It's simple, really. Inherent in our programming is the unique ability to experience what the mind believes to be true.

Our feelings of shame are the source of all forms of self-sabotage and self-punishment. We do bad things and become our own worst enemies because we feel bad about ourselves, because we don't feel worthy of the success, the stardom, the adoration, the pleasure, or the love that we have or that we desire. The fear that we are undeserving, that we will no longer belong to the club if we have too much, or just the opposite—that we won't be loved if we have too little—drives us to sabotage our success. It doesn't matter which of these you feel the most shame around; they are two sides of the same coin. Feeling unworthy and undeserving of the good in our lives, we do something—consciously or unconsciously—to punish ourselves. It's part of the human experience.

Regardless of the facades we show the world, whether we want to admit it or not, we all know we're not perfect. We know what we do behind closed doors, and we know what we've done in the past to others and ourselves. We know the viciousness of our judgments and the harshness of our prejudices. We know that underneath it all we are not that good, so we have to throw in a little sabotage to remind ourselves and others that we are just another messed-up human being. When we are reminded of the fact that we are less fortunate, less attractive, less educated, less talented, or less desirable than those around us, we punish ourselves. And likewise, whenever we are confronted with the fact that we have more brains, beauty, creativity, money, luck, or talent than those around us and we don't know how to process it our guilt drives us to do something that will bring us down. Why? Because we are ashamed, not just of the bad parts of ourselves but the good as well. How crazy is this? How absolutely insane is it to be a human being? Here we are, scared to death of being bad and then at the same time scared to death of being too great. Here we are, ashamed of what we are and ashamed of what we are not. Even if we manage to create a certain degree of success, love, money, adoration, and respect, if we don't heal our shame, make peace with our past, and find our inherent self-worth, we will inevitably create some circumstance to punish ourselves.

Once you understand this, you can begin to deactivate this programming and you will no longer have to shame yourself. To heal, you have to be able to distinguish this programming and acknowledge its existence. It can hurt you only when it's left unattended and is lurking in the recesses of your subconscious mind.

5

THE FALLOUT
OF FEAR

Having been shamed for some aspect of our character or our behavior, each of us creates a smoke screen that hides from the outside world the deep and tormenting shame we feel inside. When we realize we will not be loved or approved of if we allow our authentic expression to just hang out, we begin the pain-filled journey of covering it up.

All of us harbor some form of this primal fear. We see ourselves as standing on the outside looking in, wanting desperately to belong but fearing we're not good enough to be a part of the pack. We fear being labeled the black sheep, a reject, and we hunger to be liked, to be respected, and, most of all, to belong. We want to be picked for the team, asked to the prom, and voted most popular. We want to be Mom's golden boy and Daddy's little girl. We don't want people to find out that our father is out of work, our brother is in prison, or our mother is a raging alcoholic. We don't want to be the only Jew in a classroom of Christians, the only Mexican in a neighborhood of whites, or the only gay in a world we imagine is straight. We want to belong. We want to be chosen. We want to fit in and be wanted. We want to be loved and accepted, and when we aren't, we feel deeply ashamed and afraid.

The fear that we won't be loved or accepted if we show our true self comes from the deep shame we feel inside. And this shame stems from the belief that our authentic self is inherently and hopelessly flawed. Fear is one of the main drivers of all our deviant or so-called bad behaviors, and it manifests itself in countless ways—fear of not being liked, not being seen, or not being special. It shows up as a fear of failure, of being out of control, of not being taken care of, of being hurt or abandoned, of being exposed, of not fitting in, of being put down, of being betrayed, of being wrong, or of somebody taking what's ours. Fear has us close ourselves off and fight for what we think we need, even if in doing so we bring about our own demise. It is this primal fear that triggers our most destructive thoughts and gives rise to our most toxic emotions: hurt, hopelessness, sadness, anger, jealousy, and hate.

Our patterns of denial, suppression, and rejection are all rooted in fear. We fear that if we admit to our flaws or shortcomings, we will be labeled and then punished by our peers and loved ones. Our root insecurities are born as we discover our darker impulses and disown certain aspects of ourselves. Fearing that the voice of our shame is true, we continue to hide our weaknesses and vulnerabilities because we believe that exposing and admitting to them will give them the power to hurt us. Living in abject fear that we will be found out, we forfeit our innate right to feel good about ourselves, to say what we think, to ask for help, to take risks, and to boldly express our deepest desires.

Without fear there would be no shame, no wounded ego, and no false self—for the false self is created out of fear. It is fear that tells us to repress our human impulses such as our sexual desires, our jealousy, our selfishness, and our basic egocentric nature. It is the voice of fear that warns us that if we express our authentic self we will be shunned, disowned, and abandoned. We turn the very fear that has us separate and hide our truest selves (both our light and our dark sides) back onto ourselves, using it as a weapon to keep us small and scared. We turn away from our so-called human imperfections and vulnerabilities because we fear they are bad, dirty, or otherwise unacceptable. Every time we dissociate from an aspect of ourselves, we do so out of fear. We fear we will be ridiculed for one of our many imperfections; we fear that someone will find out about our perversions, our inadequacies, and our human scars and we'll be humiliated. So we make the decision to hide them. And with great disdain, we begin the process of disowning the totality of our humanity. We do this by dissociating ourselves from and hiding these unwanted aspects of ourselves, pretending we are not that which others—and now ourselves as well—deem inappropriate or unacceptable. We start to understand that if we are to be accepted or to fit in, we will have to figure out a way to keep these parts of ourselves disguised. But beneath this smoke screen of fear, our basic human emotions, when denied the right to be expressed, begin to fester and become toxic.

Toxic Emotions

The fallout of fear in our world is pervasive, extreme, and yet regularly minimized. Right now, on just about any city block or suburban cul-de-sac, we can find someone whose fear-based thoughts have led them to act out in inappropriate ways and sabotage some area of their life. Every act of self-sabotage is precipitated by a volatile combination of fear and one or more of our suppressed emotions that can no longer be held down or controlled. Fear is the active ingredient that arms our otherwise healthy emotions with an explosive power that inevitably leads to self-destruction.

When fear runs amok in our psyche, it changes everything. Fear fuels our emotions, charging them with an added intensity that, if left unchecked, holds the power to wreak havoc on the life we have worked so hard to create. When our emotions become infused with our primal fears—fear of loss, fear of failure, fear of emotional pain, fear of loneliness, fear of rejection, fear of not getting our needs met, fear of abandonment, fear of never finding love again, fear of public humiliation, fear of our loved ones being hurt, or fear for our basic survival—they are powerful enough to bring us to our knees.

It's imperative to understand that our emotions become problematic only when they have no healthy way to be expressed or digested. When granted the right to exist, our emotions rise and fall, surface and dissolve naturally. To witness the healthy expression of emotions, all you need to do is observe any human baby. Unless they were born into very extreme circumstances, most babies express the full range of human emotions in a very short time. One moment the baby is peaceful, the next it's scream-ing for attention, the next it's sad and crying big tears, and then it's back to cooing peacefully. In less than a minute, a healthy human being can move through the full spectrum of basic human emotions. Anger, sadness, hurt, fear, and other emotions that we later come to label as negative are actually essential modes of communication. They are feelings in motion, waves of energy seeking expression. When we are infants and small chil-dren, our emotions allow us to "say" what we don't have words for. When we become adults, our emotions bottleneck inside us when they are not allowed to move freely—whether they are subconsciously repressed or consciously withheld. Seeking ex-pression at any cost, they cause us to act out in self-destructive ways.

Our emotions are designed to act as guides that tell us what feels good and what feels bad. They're a part of our feedback system, a continuous interplay of "call and response." Our emo-tions—including our most relentless sabotaging emotions—are always leading us back to where we have made ourselves wrong or split off from the whole of who we are. They are meant to alert us when something is going on that violates our healthy nature and to let us know when something is not right. When we fail to heed the wisdom of our own feelings or become unwilling to let them move through us, they build up and become dangerous. The suppression of what was once a healthy emotion renders it toxic. Like lava, the toxic emotions beneath the surface of our conscious awareness, if left uncared for, will erupt, causing us to act out in some destructive way. Our repressed emotions taint our thought processes and hijack our better judgment, and then a negative treadmill starts to roll: toxic thoughts direct our emotions, toxic emotions inform our thoughts again, and we're soon caught in a destructive, circular pattern that gains momentum and must eventually seek a release.

Underneath every destructive act we will find a toxic buildup of one or more unexpressed emotions. If we are brave enough to identify the emotions that lurk beneath our own uncontrollable bad behavior, we can get at the root of the problem and begin to deactivate the potential bombs that lie before us. Only by accepting our emotions can we effectively disarm them; to the extent that we repress them, we will be at their mercy.

Toxic Emotion No. 1: Hurt

Unexpressed, unattended, and unhealed hurt becomes a toxic emotion that lies at the heart of why good people do bad things. It is one of the most underestimated sources of self-sabotage at work in our inner lives. When we are honest with ourselves, most of us can remember when and how we have been hurt. All we have to do is look back at times in our lives that we wish hadn't happened and we will be present to some of the unwanted and painful experiences we've endured. We've all been hurt by things that were said and not said, by things that were done and not done. Unbeknownst to us, these hurtful moments shaped and defined who we are.

I see it time after time as I lead people through deep emotional-release processes. It doesn't matter if someone is a corporate CEO, a spiritual leader, a professional athlete, a stay-at-home mom, or an administrative assistant; when we peel away the layers of our most damaging beliefs, attitudes, emotions, habits, and behaviors, we find that there is a wound to the heart that has never been fully acknowledged, cared for, integrated, and healed. Look beneath the layers of shame, fear, hopelessness, sadness, guilt, jealousy, anger, rage, hate, and other devastating emotions that destroy lives, and you will always find a hurt (or succession of hurts) that has left a wound that has been covered over without having received proper care.

When we are hurt, we often seek to hurt others, whether we are aware of it or not. If we've been ripped off, criticized, or rejected by another, we will knowingly or unknowingly seek ways to inflict this very hurt on others, as though by causing someone else hurt we could take away some of our own. In a vast majority of cases, those who sexually assault children—whether through molestation, flashing, or consuming child pornography—were once sexually violated themselves and are now perpetuating the abuse in an attempt to ease their own pain.

Most of us have learned to apply countless Band-Aids to cover our hurt, placing our attention on any number of things we hope will provide a momentary diversion from our pain. Relationships, children, friendships, careers, financial acquisition, travel, and to-do lists may distract us for a while, but the hurts we've endured do not always heal with the passage of time. Often they hold great lessons to be learned, and until we revisit them and extract the wisdom that they hold, we will continue to be used by a wound of our past and driven to act out in ways that don't even make sense to us. Although buried in the recesses of our subconscious, our unprocessed hurts are very much alive and, like a homing device, will seek out quick fixes in the form of indulgent behaviors that our subconscious believes will make us feel better. Unresolved hurt is at the root of all addictive and compulsive behaviors. And when compounded by our fear of confronting the incidents that have wounded us in the first place, it sets us up to re-wound ourselves by doing hurtful things to ourselves and others.

Fear compounds the hurt we've endured in a way that is so pervasive, so insidious, that most of us don't even recognize that the compounding has occurred. Fear sets us up to *expect* more hurt, to anticipate the moment the other shoe will drop, and robs us of trust, vulnerability, and intimacy. Hurt, when intensified by the fear that we'll be hurt again in the future, gives birth to countless negative expectations—expectations that lead to self-sabotage and disappointment. Unacknowledged hurt creates a circular path that leads to both victimhood and further victimization.

Toxic Emotion No. 2: Hopelessness

Fear joins with resignation to create a state of hopelessness, where we no longer believe we have the ability to create a life of meaning and success, or to break free from the messes we've created. Hopelessness strips us of our self-confidence and blinds us to the possibilities and opportunities that are right in front of us. Without hope we are left with only the painfully limited prospects of our wounded egos. Hopelessness leads to insane acts of self-destruction, because without hope, we no longer consider or even care about the consequences of our choices. Hopeless people pick up guns and shoot other people or act out on an array of other dark impulses, grasping for a momentary fix through which they can reconnect and feel hopeful again. The random crimes and violence perpetrated by addicts, smugglers, and gang members are all born of hopelessness. Hopelessness is dangerous because it seduces us into not giving a crap about the pain that our actions may cause. In its throes we are driven to hurt others and ourselves in an attempt to find a life raft—some temporary flotation device—to keep us from drowning in our sorrow.

If we stop to examine our lives, we can often see where and when we gave up on ourselves—where and when we decided we were no good, unworthy, and incapable of having a happy and successful life. We can see where we began to withdraw from our hopes and dreams, whether we withdrew from having intimate love, from becoming a respected and contributory member of society, from acquiring financial stability, from having the career we dreamed of, or from attaining another important goal. If our hopelessness remains unaddressed, we will continue to be at risk of selling our souls, our integrity, and our dignity.

Toxic Emotion No. 3: Sadness

Healthy sadness is a necessary emotion. It gives our hearts a way to grieve, accept, and ultimately move through life's disappointments. At a deep level, sadness and sorrow intermingle, allowing us to mourn the loss of that which we have loved. But when we are clobbered with loss that we can't understand or refuse to let go of, sadness can cloud our vision and cause us to shut down. The haze of suppressed sadness inhibits our ability to give and receive love, count our blessings, and enjoy our lives.

When fueled by the fear that we will never be happy or whole again, sadness can turn into an abyss of self-pity. Fear turns the cleansing nature of genuine sorrow into a self-indulgent and myopic focus on our own failures and losses, which leads to self-absorption. Sadness eats away at our emotional well-being when it spirals into depression and despondency.

Sad people believe they are bad and usually blame themselves for their heartache, and although this emotion is less likely to cause us to harm another, it most certainly causes us to hurt ourselves. Unprocessed, toxic sadness leads us to commit horrible crimes against ourselves—the most severe of which is suicide. Sad people drink too much, eat too much, gamble or spend too much, or indulge themselves in an array of other addictions to mask their pain. Recent statistics show that in the United States alone, over 18 million people are taking antidepressant medications in an attempt to pull themselves out of the dark hole of a saddened heart. Countless others are finding alternative ways to medicate themselves. Too often, though, these medications are nothing more than a Band-Aid for the sadness that lives inside us. Rather than providing a healthy outlet for our emotions, these medications merely allow it to build up unnoticed until some self-sabotaging incident triggers its release. When we refuse to allow sadness to move through us, it claims our vitality, our energy, and, sometimes, our lives.

Toxic Emotion No. 4: Anger

Most of us live in denial of the amount of unexpressed and undigested anger we carry around with us on a daily basis. Although we may not be screaming obscenities at our children or punching holes in walls, our anger wears an astonishing array of masks—from overt hostility on one end of the spectrum to mild impatience on the other.

Healthy anger gives us access to our power as autonomous and free adults. It allows us to assert our boundaries and protect ourselves and others. Anger can spur us to action when it's time to take a stand and have our voice be heard. It's a natural and healthy response when we've been hurt, abused, taken advantage of, betrayed, or deceived. But when our anger is undigested and unprocessed, it builds up and shoots out of us in a variety of destructive ways. It's the voice that screams, "I'll do what I want when I want!" Pent-up, toxic anger is the trigger that makes us lash out at our partners, break things in a rage, become reckless behind the wheel, and abuse those we love.

When we're afraid, anger is a natural response system—a defense mechanism, like a tiger bearing its claws. But when fueled by too much fear and compounded by shame, healthy anger amasses into a weapon of destruction rather than a source of power and protection. Fear is the active ingredient that renders our anger explosive. The fear that we won't get our needs met, that we'll be taken advantage of, or that we'll be betrayed or humiliated gives us a target for our unexpressed anger.

In its mildest forms, anger can show up as procrastination, sarcasm, teasing, gossiping, criticizing those around us, or sulking. In its more dangerous form, anger can cause resentments to harden into grudges, irritation to turn into road rage, and passive-aggressiveness (as if that weren't bad enough) to morph into overt and unwanted acts of violence. At its worst, unattended anger destroys us and annihilates all in its pain.

Toxic Emotion No. 5: Jealousy

Jealousy is the outward projection of our inner insecurities. Born out of feelings that we are unwanted, unworthy of love, or not special enough and out of the fear that we are about to lose something we have claimed as ours, jealousy is an internal fire whose flames can quickly grow, causing us to lash out in mean and vindictive ways, inciting temporary insanity, and driving good people to do all sorts of bad things. In his essay "On Life and Sex," the British psychologist Havelock Ellis said, "Jealousy is the dragon which slays love under the pretense of keeping it alive." In an instant, jealousy can destroy the lives of all those in its path.

The fear that we will never have the talent, affection, love, or material possessions that we desire drives this often well-hidden emotion to the surface. We feel jealous when we think someone has something we should have. We feel jealous when we believe we'll never have or get what we want in life. We feel jealous when we judge our own self to be insufficient and yearn to be something more than we are. We feel jealous when those around us appear to have talents, gifts, or opportunities greater than our own. Feeling less than those around us is the Achilles' heel of the jealous person. After coming up with the short end of the stick over and over again, and feeling as though we somehow got a raw deal, we can no longer suppress our jealousy, and we lash out in an act of vengeance. This bitter cocktail of jealousy, inadequacy, and anger can appear as indifference, pettiness, criticism, or meanness.

Jealousy drives good people to do horrible things: Fathers hurt the mothers of their children and vice versa. Scorned lovers destroy property or set up traps for those who don't return their affections. Family feuds that could easily be mended go unresolved for years. Jealous ex-employees create computer viruses or file frivolous lawsuits for the sole purpose of hurting and disrupting the lives of those they believe have something that they do not.

Jealousy has also been described as "the ulcer of the soul." It is a corrupting and debilitating emotion that erodes our self-worth and transfers our feelings of inadequacy onto the face of its victims. Each of us who has felt overtaken by jealousy's wrath at any time already knows its potential to quickly drive us to be our own worst enemy.

Toxic Emotion No. 6: Hate

No matter how we dress it up, hate is recognizable by its intensity. Whether expressed as meanness, vengeance, bigotry, racism, or hostility, hate is a toxic brew of anger, fear, and rejection. Usually arising out of a past marked by some type of abuse or neglect, hate becomes a way to project onto others the horrible feelings we have no way to digest.

An emotion of extremes, hate is completely ruled by fear. Intense and uncontrollable fear drives hate and amplifies its destructiveness, turning gossip into defamation, avoidance into neglect, insults into degradation, dislike into repulsion, anger into rage, intimidation into violence, and spite into cruelty.

Hate aims to remove or destroy the one who is hated. When projected outward, it seeks to instill fear in the person who is hated—even when the person who is hated is ourselves. Self-hatred perpetuates a vicious cycle: We attempt to deaden the pain with addictions of all kinds—addictions to drama, drugs, alcohol, food, spending, struggling, and suffering, to name a few. The further we dive into the cesspool of addiction, the more we hate ourselves and anyone else we blame for our condition.

The cost of hating ourselves and others is staggering and far-reaching. Hate is the culprit behind war, religious crimes, bigotry, gay-bashing, vandalizing, and slave labor. On a personal level, hate robs us of our self-respect, dignity, strength, power, and the one thing we are all seeking—love.

The Devastation of Toxic Emotions

As we have seen, our natural, normal human emotions—when fueled by fear and suffocated by suppression—become an explosive mix that can ignite at any moment and destroy our lives. When we don't allow ourselves to feel and then express our feelings, we become victims of our own denied emotions and held hostage by our fear. Often we don't even realize what is brewing just beneath the surface until the damage has already been done. Here is a case in point.

Sam S. is a thirty-two-year-old military man whose early history of neglect and abuse left him deeply wounded. Because he was raised in a household where "boys don't cry," Sam tried to keep his emotions under control by becoming rigid and highly structured. He planned his days, weeks, and months in order to ensure himself the future he desired. He knew what kind of wife he desired from an early age, and when he finally identified the perfect woman—the one who fit into his well-laid-out plan—Sam directed her family to plan the perfect wedding. Months later, right on schedule, his wife got pregnant, and together they began creating the perfect family.

Sam and his beautiful wife, Sarah, went to church on Sundays, followed by a few hours of family time. They had their nightly dinners at home right at 6:45 P.M., even if it was inconvenient or caused utter chaos. Everything had to be just as Sam wanted and needed it to be in order to feel in control and at ease. Then one day, when Sarah could no longer tolerate his controlling behavior, her pent-up anger took over, and, without thinking, she began looking for ways to relieve her own pain. It wasn't long before Sarah began to have an affair with a neighbor's husband. Months later, when Sam unexpectedly came home from work one day because he was feeling sick, Sam found Sarah in bed with her lover, flew out of control, beat him nearly to death, and, of course, was arrested and charged with attempted murder. In an instant, Sam's perfectly controlled life was destroyed. Never was this act thought about, nor were the consequences considered. When he could no longer control his outer world and what he felt inside, all his pent-up and unhealed emotions exploded in a moment of rage. This all-loving, all-American boy shocked his friends, family, and colleagues. No one knew, no one suspected—another good boy gone bad.

James A. was a highly respected dentist and an active member of several nonprofit organizations. He grew up in a household where his father constantly berated his mother, putting her down, treating her with disrespect, and humiliating her. James, feeling powerless to do anything to help his mother, began beating himself up daily with feelings of guilt and remorse. He hated that he was not man enough to stand up to his father and protect his mother. The only way he could cope was to become numb inside. He looked for and eventually found ways to suppress his painful and dark emotions. After years of repression, his despair led him to a fascination with pornography and a lust for twelve-year-old girls. The very week he became elected to the board of a prominent charity, police tied his address to a child pornography ring, blowing the lid off James's longtime perversion. As his double life was exposed, it ripped his family apart, separating him from his three young kids, his wife, and everything he had worked so hard to build. In James's case, his release—and ultimately his downfall—was through pornography. Toxic emotions will always find a release.

Our shame demands that we cover up our fear and put on a mask so no one will find out the truth about us. But of one thing we can be sure: if we don't deal with our fear and our toxic emotions, one day they will deal with us. Then the truth about ourselves that we never wanted to see or have seen will be exposed.

6

THE EGO
GONE BAD

The ego in and of itself is not a dark force. It is a necessity for us to have an ego if we want to function in the world. The personality-driven side of our being isn't intrinsically bad or wrong; it has an important role to play in our everyday lives. In fact, without a healthy ego we would end up in a mental institution because we would not be able to distinguish ourselves from others. Although many believe that being a spiritual person means getting rid of or getting out of our ego, when properly understood and used, our ego actually supports us in our journey to explore our talents and develop our unique gifts. Our healthy ego helps us assert ourselves, draw boundaries, and know ourselves as individuals. The ego is the force that enables us to identify with our unique body and mind. Its function is to safeguard and protect the entity that we know to be ourselves. It helps us to distinguish between what is "me" and what is "not me." Because of our healthy ego, we have the sense that we exist as individual beings.

In its healthiest state, the ego adores life, which is why it appoints itself as the governor of our life and affairs. It is responsible for creating, maintaining, and protecting our sense of self, ensuring that we continue to live and thrive. Our ego is what charges us with the deep impulse to ensure our own survival at all costs. We need a healthy ego in order to bring forth our own unique expression. And our ego needs the loving oversight of our higher self, its divine counterpart, in order to function in the way it was intended and to support us in creating lives that are meaningful and fulfilled. When the ego gets damaged, broken, hurt, and split off from its divine counterpart, it can no longer be properly used. Then, instead of being beneficial to our human experience, it becomes a detriment that needs constant managing. When the ego becomes distorted and no longer able to recognize itself for what it is, it becomes the main force that leads to our demise.

The Birth of the Wounded Ego

Now, you might be wondering, "How does our healthy ego become wounded and this distortion occur?" The wounded ego takes form when something happens that makes it feel less than—when something threatens it, beats it, berates it, ignores it, rejects it, molests it, or abandons it. There are tens of thousands of different incidents people go through that can prove to be just too much for their healthy ego to digest. So at some point, when the pain is too much to bear, the healthy ego begins to separate from the intelligence of the whole self and becomes its own force to be reckoned with—thus the birth of the wounded ego.

The once healthy ego, wanting to dissociate itself from its damaged or wounded aspects, begins to push those parts of itself out of its line of sight in the attempt to make them go away. Thinking that if it hides its flaws and imperfections, its insecurities, mistakes, shame, and wounds, deep enough, no one will discover the ugly truth—not even the ego itself—and it will be safe. This is how the break from our integrated, whole self gradually occurs. Let me give you an example.

Your healthy ego enrolls you in business school, fueled by the desire to become the head of a Fortune 500 company that is a world leader in its field. Your healthy ego drives you to excel in your classes, learn how to debate, read up on all the latest and most innovative business techniques, and study people who are highly successful and at the top of their careers. When you graduate, you land a great job at one of these Fortune 500 companies and begin to climb the corporate ladder.

Then one day you realize there are many others who are also on the same chase to get to the top (the ego can always sense competition), and you become anxious. Your healthy ego is now threatened by the realization that you may not have what it takes to succeed. This thought triggers some hidden shame that you are not as smart as everyone else. Suddenly you feel you can't just sit back and go about business in the usual way. So you have to ramp it up, as they say. You start to look at what you have heard and seen about how to climb to the top, and you begin to make different choices—choices informed by your shame and based in fear. Maybe you start socializing with people you don't feel that good about. Maybe you discover that if you stretched the truth a bit you would look better in the eyes of your superiors, or that if you "borrowed" someone's idea, claiming it as your own, you would win a promotion.

Even though you might have some uncomfortable feelings about what you are doing, you rationalize your behavior, probably unconsciously, and continue on the wounded ego's path to victory. After days, months, or years of feeling conflicted by the cautionary feelings that might be whispering, "Don't do that" or "Are you sure this is OK?" you manage to override them, and then suddenly they are gone, forever buried. The wounded ego has now invaded the boundaries of the healthy ego, staking its claim on its territory.

The Invasion of the Wounded Ego

When the unhealthy ego senses a bit of danger, it automatically searches for distractions, working diligently to protect its territory, which is now all of *you*. Even though it began as only part of you, because of its deceptive nature and your inability to distinguish it from your authentic self, which encompasses both the ego and your eternal essence, it has become the only "you" that you know. Although at times you might have a moment of heightened awareness in which you want to make a higher choice, you unknowingly weigh that wisdom against the voice of your now wounded ego. And more than likely you will make the lower choice, because your wounded ego has already done so much internal damage that its voice has become the only one you can hear. It shouts out:

How can I be sure?

I can't trust anyone.

There is nobody there for me.

It's a dog-eat-dog world.

Screw them! I've worked hard for everything I have. No one gave me any breaks!

There are no free rides.

There are only two certainties in life: death and taxes.

I've been hurt before, and I'm not taking any more chances.

Nobody knows the pain I've endured.

They don't care about me.

It won't make a difference anyway.

I'm entitled to whatever I want.

What a bunch of crap!

I'm not as sick as they are.

Look how far I've come.

This won't work for me.

They've made their bed; now they've got to lie in it.

They're a bunch of idiots, and I don't need to listen to them.

I'm getting what I deserve.

The voice of your wounded ego, like an animal in pain, grows so loud over time that it drowns out the higher voice of reason and causes you to ignore your higher self. It has you shut the door on the totality of who you are and focus on what's wrong and what's missing. When the ego is wounded, it refuses to see, listen to, or hear any truth other than the one voiced by itself. This is its main defense mechanism. For it to survive it must be right about the way it sees itself, others, and the world at large. It must, without the shadow of a doubt, search out and manufacture realities, circumstances, and situations that are consistent with its beliefs about the world. The job of the wounded ego is now to protect itself at all costs and to block out anything that can cause it to feel the deep shame and pain that created the wound in the first place.

When the unhealthy ego takes over, it becomes a loose wire, dangerous and out of control. Once wounded, the ego loses its ability to distinguish fact from fiction, reality from drama. As a protection mechanism, the wounded ego becomes self-focused. When the wounded ego is running the show, or your entire life, it's because it has succeeded in masking your higher nature, disconnecting you from at least half of who you are. The ego is a master warrior and has many mechanisms to ensure its victory. It works diligently to protect its turf and to hide the higher aspects of self so that it may prevail. The unhealthy ego's main defense, and ultimately its downfall, is arrogance. "I am bigger and better," it says. "The rules don't apply to me. I can do what I want, and no one will find out." In all its righteousness it screams, "No one can tell me what to do!" Or even worse, in a soft whisper it purports, "No one will know. No one will find out."

These are all messages of the unhealthy ego and the voice of separateness. The wounded ego truly believes that it can act in accordance with its own laws and get away with it. So it does—thus the birth of self-sabotage. If the rules don't apply to me, then I can and will do what I want, when I want to do it. While the healthy ego's function is to give us a separate and unique identity, the unhealthy ego takes this a step farther, seeking to prove that we are unique and special even if it overrides our integrity, violates other people's boundaries, or breaks the law.

When the wounded ego is running the show, the outer world is seen only as something to fulfill its needs and make it feel better. Other people show up either as potential bandages for the wound, as problems to be solved, or as obstacles to be conquered. The wounded ego, acting separately from the greater whole, is now like a fish out of water—flopping around uncontrollably, trying to find its way back to safety. Lost and alone in this debilitating separateness, it searches for ways to make sense out of its life. But instead of seeing itself as being a part of the greater whole, it can see only what it doesn't have. It loses the ability to see the big picture and can see only through the narrow perspective of its limited self—alone, small, and seemingly abandoned. In the desperate attempt to regain control, it steps into the lead role, casting itself as the star of the show. Suddenly the most desperate, flawed, and wounded part of us is in control. The massive invasion by the cancerous wounded ego has begun.

The Ego's Desperate Quest for Approval

The pain of our wounded ego drives us to be different from who we are. We fight to be bigger, stronger, tougher, and more secure. We position ourselves to show that we are more, better, or different than the rest of the crowd. We run around like chickens without heads, scrambling to create a persona that we believe will bring us the greatest amount of love, approval, and the recognition that we desperately need. We act and behave in ways, consciously or unconsciously, that will leave others with the thoughts, feelings, and impressions that we believe will bring us the most respect and approval. We are driven to behave, whether we like this fact or not, in order to get some internal need met. We are mandated by our wounded ego to act and perform for the "food" (i.e., the emotional fix) we need. The ego's food is love, acknowledgment, recognition, flattery, appreciation, approval, and respect—anything that tells it that it's OK.

Michelle B. was a talented designer who apprenticed for a well-known architect in the Midwest. After a falling-out with her boss, Michelle lost her job but decided to keep her former title on her business card. Fearing that otherwise nobody would hire her and that she would never get the respect her wounded ego needed, she passed herself off as an architect. She got away with this deception, lying time after time, and took on projects that were outside the scope of her training. Eventually, after costing dozens of homeowners hundreds of thousands of dollars and being sued five times, she was brought to justice. An ego wounded and on the chase will stop at nothing in its attempt to fill the void left by being separated from its true essence.

Because the ego feels incomplete and inferior without its healthy counterpart, it is constantly comparing and assessing how it is doing, how it's holding up in what it perceives to be the battle called life. The wounded ego feeds off feeling better than the next guy or gal, being prettier, smarter, sexier, skinnier, richer, more desirable, more educated, or more powerful. It craves more and more of whatever it believes will make it feel as good as or better than the next guy.

The wounded ego wants to win the big prize, at all costs. Like a parasite, it keeps devouring its host, even though this action will result in its eventual demise. The insatiable hunger for "more, better, and different" than what it has comes from how deeply it's been wounded, as does its intense desire to fit in and belong. When the ego is wounded, it desperately tries to repair itself by creating outer circumstances that will make it feel better. Feeling inherently damaged, flawed, and inadequate, the wounded ego grasps at things outside itself to make it whole. Some wounded egos will slip into the trance of materialism, thinking that if they acquire enough "things" they will prove their worth, while others will try to summon a sense of self-worth through flirtation and seduction, being desired by and winning the attention of others. Some will find momentary solace in being needed, while others will figure out ways to gain power. This is how the great chase begins—the chase to prove that we are someone other than who we believe ourselves to be, the chase to find outer things to cover up our emotions, the chase to outrun our feelings of shame and the deeply rooted inner turmoil we keep hidden within us. All this energy expended just so we don't have to feel the deep shame of our own human flaws, imperfections, and vulnerabilities.

The nature of the emotional wounds that caused the split in the first place will determine what each person's ego will seek to relieve its pain. Based on its unique needs and desires, the wounded ego will develop particular strategies to make itself feel better. Some egos are structured to believe money is the solution, so they will chase money as the cure for their wounds, even if that means embezzling, robbing, cheating, or participating in crimes of passion or lust. Inside of other ego structures, power is believed to be the cure, so these people will go after the prestige of positions where they are the head honcho. Some will try to feel better by dominating, manipulating, controlling, and conquering others, leading to behaviors ranging from infidelity to sex crimes, from lying to blackmail. The ego truly believes it will feel better and return to wholeness by gathering these outer experiences. It does all of this in hopes that it will satisfy its hunger and meet its need to feel loved and approved of.

The unhealthy ego seeks instant gratification and quick feel-good moments. Consequences are not even considered or understood, because the arrogance of the distorted ego creates a separation between fantasy and reality that renders us blind to our own behavior. And herein lies the danger: when we cannot see ourselves, when we can no longer recognize the impact of our own behavior, we become vulnerable to being a slave to our unhealthy ego's distorted desires.

Without the balance of the higher self, the wounded ego is on a continual quest to prove that it is more important, respected, admired, and successful than everyone else. But here is the conundrum: No matter what the wounded ego manages to get or achieve, at the end of the day it still falls short. My friend and mentor Suzanne West explains this psychological state as "the failure of the Wishing Tree, which occurs when our hungry egos are on the chase for the next brass ring, seeking the next IT (whatever 'it' may be), and thinking that satisfying the next desire will fill our emotional holes and bring us the long-eluded joy and fulfillment that we are looking for." But I can assure you, no matter how much the ego achieves in the outer world, what it really longs for does not exist outside itself; it exists in the inner world. The ego is ultimately seeking to return, to be reunited with its counterpart. In this it is never fulfilled, no matter how many successes it experiences, how many compliments it elicits, or how many material possessions it gathers. Because in comparison to our whole integrated self, the wounded ego fails miserably. So in its desperate attempt to measure up, the only option it sees is to go after what it believes will balance out the scales and make it an equal. The unbearable thought of being "less than" is the wounded ego's drive.

Herein lies the fundamental problem and the source of most of our everyday neuroses: The wounded ego *is* "less than" when compared to its divine counterpart. It's downright flawed, imperfect, needy, defective, angry, manipulating, controlling, greedy, self-absorbed, judging, criticizing, power hungry, and defensive, and exhibits a huge array of other unattractive qualities that our higher self does not identify as good or bad or right or wrong. The damaged ego lives for what it and others think. It lives for approval, for love, and for acceptance, whereas our higher self is whole unto itself, perfect, and doesn't want for more because it is unlimited, pure, and authentic. It doesn't need your or anyone else's approval because it is whole and complete and so never has to look for anything outside itself.

This higher self is whole and complete; it needs no real introduction because it doesn't even care if it is seen or recognized. That is part of the cosmic paradox. The higher self is perfect even in the presence of imperfection; it's always there, even when we are turning our backs on it. It's ever-present, never abandoning us, never swaying in its commitment to uphold our highest expression, never rushing us to transform or come home. Our eternal self is always there with our best interest at heart, even when our lower self is committed to self-destruction.

Our ego structure is so tough, so resilient, and so thick that even when the light of our higher self slips into our awareness and wakes us up, we quickly create some kind of limitation (in the form of everyday problems or self-sabotage) to cover up our most unified and limitless self. Nothing is harder for us than to let go of our ego's "safe" and predictable thoughts, beliefs, behaviors, and comforts. It's so difficult to give up the self that we know—the wounded ego's limited and false view of the world—for the limitless possibilities that we cannot and do not know exist. This is because, once damaged, the ego, by its nature, wants and needs to have absolute control. It believes itself to be the almighty power, the supreme force, the be-all and end-all.

The ego may eventually come to know and appreciate the beauty, power, and gifts of the higher self, but more than likely it will not care unless, of course, this knowledge can help further its own self-serving cause. When we are deeply rooted in our wounded egos, we don't listen. We really don't want to know anything that might threaten our present reality or cause us feelings of discomfort or shame. We deny this abiding part of ourselves and ignorantly go about being fixated on our outer experience—what need we can get met by someone around us, and what we can get materially, physically, or emotionally. When we are under the control of our wounded ego, the inner world seems like the booby prize, unless of course paying attention to the inner world will somehow serve the ego to get its needs met.

The ultimate job of the healthy ego is to distinguish itself from the egos of others in order to confirm its reality. But the unhealthy or wounded ego believes that the best way to do this is by being right about everything, even if being right will bring some unwanted result. For example, your mother may have told you, directly or indirectly, that you were weren't good enough. When you were two, three, or five, you unconsciously bought into this belief. Because you are a well-trained human machine, you concluded that people who believe they are not good enough do not succeed, so you try to cover up this part of yourself, the part of yourself that your mother was talking about. Believing that being not good enough is wrong, you separate from this part of yourself and begin the process of creating a false self so that no one will find out the truth about who you are. So now, years later, after recycling that belief in your mind over and over again consciously or unconsciously, you go out into the world and try to do something that will prove to yourself that, in fact, both your mother's words and that haunting belief you have carried around for years were *right*. Let me give you an example.

Lory was a clingy and needy young child. She loved her mother and never wanted to leave her side. Her mother constantly berated her for how clingy she was: "You're just going to be hanging around me forever. The umbilical cord will never be broken." When Lory was a teen she did everything to prove her independence, to prove that she didn't need her mother and that she could cut the cord between them. But as she grew older and her defenses dropped, Lory began to lean on her mother again. Over the years Lory noticed how many great opportunities she was willing to let pass her by if it meant leaving the town where her mother lived.

Lory finally came to me when she was about to break off an engagement because her fiancé was being transferred to another state. Even though she worked from home and was able to live anywhere in the United States, she felt angry that her fiancé would choose to further his career and move her away from her mother. She threw a fit and wound up hitting him, caused a series of bad fights she felt she had no control over, and broke off her relationship with the love of her life. She was now ashamed and embarrassed that she had ever gotten physically abusive with anyone. She thought of herself as a calm, docile type and had never before shown any signs of being abusive with anyone, not even her bratty little brother.

Her rage had never surfaced before, and she couldn't understand what was driving her behavior. When I asked Lory if she liked living in the city she was in, she quickly said no. When I asked her if she had ever thought about moving, she said, "All the time." I wanted to know what brought up so much rage in her that she would beat up a man she loved. She had a very gentle persona and an easygoing nature. But when she answered me, she seemed to regress to being five or six years old. In a very young voice, she said she couldn't leave because her mother was right: she would never be able to cut the umbilical cord. Even though Lory did not consciously choose this belief or even want it, it was ingrained in her subconscious mind, and, by God, she was going to be right about it, even if it destroyed the rest of her life and robbed her of the love she had always dreamed about.

For Lory to move on and have a successful life, not only would she have to be wrong about her underlying belief (i.e., that she could never cut the umbilical cord): she would also have to allow her mother, whom she idolized, to be wrong as well. The wounded ego, in all its arrogance, can't seem to admit to being wrong, unless of course it gets to be right about how wrong it is.

Herein lies the issue. You can say to yourself, "I don't want to be right about the negative beliefs that make up my false self and are hidden in my subconscious mind," but emotionally you are tied to the belief structure that has created your false self. You can't help it. It's out of your control, because you have made an unconscious agreement. Since you are in the grips of your wounded ego, which believes it is the highest order, the Supreme Being, the Big Kahuna, you can't admit that you have no control over the ingrained, unconscious, shame-filled impulses of your subconscious mind. So you create a false persona—a mask, so to speak—to hide your inadequacies, your insecurities, and your deep-seated fears of being unworthy and unlovable.

7

CRACKING
THE CODE OF THE
FALSE SELF

Fear and shame are the parents of the false self. Our wounded ego, in an effort to distance itself from its deep feelings of unworthiness and powerlessness, constructs a mask, a persona, to hide behind. This false self is charged with one mission only: to hide all of the unwanted and unacceptable parts of ourselves. We wouldn't need to create a false self if at our core we felt good about who we are. We create this persona only as a way to hide and protect what others (and then we ourselves) have made wrong, bad, and unacceptable. We create a false self in the hopes that somehow it will help us fit into the strict guidelines of our outer surroundings, no matter how crazy, scary, or dull they might have been.

As children, the more we expressed ourselves, the more behaviors we displayed that were met with harsh criticism or senseless punishment, the more we separated from our true essence. With every incident that was met with disapproval, every expression that was squelched because we were crying, screaming, asking too many questions, or running around joyfully giggling while our parents were trying to work, we unconsciously separated from our authentic self, our true self. And in doing so, we also separated from our joy, from our passion, and from our ever-loving hearts. So, to ensure our emotional survival, we began the heartless process of trying to cover up our authentic self in order to become who we believed would be the "right" us, the acceptable us, the us that would belong. With each rejection, we created more and more internal separation, building thicker and thicker invisible walls to protect our sensitive and tender hearts. Day by day, experience after experience, we unknowingly constructed an invisible fortress that became our false self. This fortress of false expression—limited expression—obscured our essence, hiding our vulnerabilities, our sensitivities, and often our ability to know and see the truth about ourselves.

By the time I was ten, after a few unfortunate incidents, a big dose of rejection, and some bad decisions on my part, this corruption had occurred within me. It began as disappointment over what I perceived to be the injustices of my life and the world, and as it grew, my sweet nature was gradually replaced by a defensive stance toward others. Over time I went from sweet to bitter, from tender to tough, from open to shut down, from confident to insecure. *Stupid* was my greatest nemesis—the thing I never wanted to be. My big sister, Arielle, was both my hero and my competition, and seemed to have got all the brains when they were being handed out. Even though my grades weren't that bad, Arielle had the pizzazzy writing style, and she was the one who walked in the house with her head held high, waving her report card around so we would all stop and take notice. Standing tall and feeling self-assured, Arielle easily won the gold metal for being the smarter sister. I resigned myself to being the stupid one, which wounded my already fragile ego. It didn't take long before my divine essence and inner beauty were covered by shame and fear. I felt ashamed of being flawed, imperfect, less than, and not good enough, and I was terrified that if I exposed this weakness, I would be shunned and left out.

These wounds covered my innocence and separated me from my most precious gift—my connection with my higher self, with God and the greater whole. By the time I was eight or nine years old I had already begun the painstaking task of trying to prove to everyone around me that I did matter, that I was good enough, and that I was smart, too. Slowly I wrapped myself in a facade of arrogance and guarded my heart with all the layers of false bravado I could whip up. Now feeling separate from the world around me and painfully alone (even though there were always people around me), I began the life-draining process of pretending to be someone other than who I was. My inner insecurity led me to create an outer mask called "know-it-all." I tried hard to make my mask believable by putting up defenses to keep out any thought, belief, or judgment from others or myself that were not in alignment with my newly constructed, human-made persona. I became righteous about all of my beliefs and opinions, forcing them on those around me, thinking that this was the way to finally prove to my damaged ego that I was as smart as my sister.

So I puffed out my chest and slipped on my newly formed mask so that I could pretend that I was someone I was not. My mask—the face of my false self—gave me access to a social persona that I deemed acceptable and that I unconsciously believed would protect my tender and sensitive heart. Then the new and improved Debbie would come to the rescue, and I could pretend, at least for the moment, that I was the girl I wanted to be rather than the girl I actually was. With my mask on I could be confident and strong—the smart one everyone would come to for advice. I could be the all-wise, all-loving one my family respected and wanted to listen to. I could be the pretty one, the popular one, and the one who didn't care what other people thought. With my false self intact, I could be free of the horribly debilitating feelings of unworthiness and stupidity and pretend that I was OK. I learned to smile, dance, be cool, and act indifferent to make the mask of my false self fit a little better. I learned to fake it, and, more important, I leaned to protect my heart (or so I thought) and hide my inadequacies. Little by little, I found ways to cover up the shame and fear I felt inside.

Internal Corruption

The only way to ensure that our authentic and flawed self will not be discovered or exposed is to start to develop the opposite side of the quality we are trying to hide. What a great cover-up. We disguise ourselves and carefully construct a mask to hide behind so that no one, not even we ourselves, will recognize us. We work hard to overcompensate with whatever quality we believe to be the positive opposite of the quality we despise. If as a child you felt like you were invisible, if you felt unseen and unrecognized by the people you loved the most, you may have adopted an attention-seeking persona to attract the attention you craved. If you felt insignificant, you may have created an outer facade that would make you feel important.

This is how it works. Desperately seeking to belong, we tried tirelessly to turn ourselves into anything we thought would be desirable to our families, friends, classmates, or other external influences that we wanted to be a part of. Without a second thought, we gave up our light, we gave up our innocence, we gave up our deepest truth, and we covered up our authentic expression. In a fight to hold on to the love that we needed, we withdrew from that which is most sacred; we ventured outside our authentic desires, and we tried to achieve the impossible: to fit in, to be approved of, to be accepted, and to be loved by those we deemed worthy of our love and affection. Voilà—the successful birth of our false self.

Our shame and fear convince us to wear an infinite number of masks to hide behind. Because we lack the understanding that not only we but our dear friends and family all possess inner demons, we deny these parts of ourselves and begin the tireless process of creating personas—costumes, so to speak—to conceal all of who we really are. We create outer facades so that no one will find out about our dark thoughts, desires, and impulses. The problem with this, of course, is that eventually we lose sight not just of our darkness but of our light as well. Our authentic nature is now covered with residue, and we begin to function entirely and mechanically from the lowest aspects of ourselves—our wounded ego.

The wounded ego, utterly convinced that it will be shunned or rejected if its imperfections are revealed, forgets that it has designed a persona, a mask, to show the world. So it inevitably loses access to its bright and more evolved counterpart and identifies itself completely with the false self that it has created. The mission of the false self is to make itself acceptable to itself, which again is a mind bender, because the false self was created to avoid dealing with the "self" it believed itself to be because of its wounds. Then this new self (the false self) tries tirelessly to be someone it's not so no one will find out the truth: that it isn't the real, authentic self, which you decided was damaged and lost decades ago.

The false self has so many ways to conceal its shame, hide its pain, and disguise its true nature. That is why it is so difficult to discover the truth about our magnificent nature and why we usually have to commit some unbelievably self-destructive act before we can break through the steely facade of our false self and crack the code that convinced us to hide our true nature in the first place.

The wounded ego can take on a variety of different masks to camouflage its perceived inadequacies. The nature of the facade that we choose varies from person to person, and most of us have more than one social mask that we wear, depending on who we are with and what stage of life we are in. Most of us began constructing these exterior facades at an early age as we tried to calculate which way of being would get us the most love and provide the greatest cover-up for our wrenching shame and our wounded egos. Some of us chose our personas by observing how others perceived our true and authentic self and then adjusting our personas accordingly. We may have chosen a particular persona thinking it would protect us from harm or make us invisible so that we would go unnoticed by those who were critical of us. We may have taken on the mask of the Tough

Guy / Tough Cookie because that's what our culture expected, or because we feared that if we exposed our sweet, innocent self, we would be beaten, taken advantage of, shunned, or teased. If stupidity was condemned in our households, we might have become the intellectual snob, otherwise known as the know-it-all.

We may have chosen a particular mask because we saw how well it worked for someone we knew. Maybe we met a friend at school who gained admiration or respect by flaunting the mask of the Good Girl, Too Cool, or the Bully, so we fashioned our persona in their likeness. We might have observed how much attention the Seductress seemed to get from men or how the Charmer always seemed to have women eating out of the palm his hand. Maybe we realized early on that we were never going to be the so-called popular one, so we opted for what we hoped would be the next best thing—becoming the Entitled Supporter and positioning ourselves close to those with fame, power, or a status higher than our own. Maybe guilt and burden were passed down from generation to generation in your family, so you just took on the persona you saw operating in your mother and became a classic martyr.

Our masks were formed through our early observations about which of our behaviors were deemed acceptable and which were not. Then we consciously, or unconsciously, began to model ourselves after what we believed would either hide our unacceptable traits or bring us the kind of love and attention we desired. Some of us were aware even at a young age that we were trying to be someone we were not, and some of us automatically, unconsciously took on a facade to hide the disowned and unacceptable parts of ourselves. Even now, some of you who are reading this will know exactly what I am taking about, while some of you may not even realize you are wearing some version of the mask that you put on twenty, thirty, or even forty years ago. And unbeknownst to you, your authentic self is hidden behind that mask. Imagine that you received a little gift—a magic penny, perhaps—from your grandmother when you were a small child. Wanting to keep it safe, you hid it somewhere so no one would find it. Would you be able to remember, all these decades later, where you had hidden it? Would you remember that you hid it at all? The same is true for our unscathed authentic self. We've kept it hidden for so long that we've forgotten who it is or that it ever existed in the first place.

Regardless of the particular facade you chose, or whether you created it consciously or unconsciously, your mask was constructed to distance you from the shame that you felt about certain aspects of your true nature. And, more important, it was constructed to ensure that those unwanted aspects remained hidden from the world.

The embarrassment that led you to create your specific mask could be one of a thousand things. For example, your shame might be that you're poor white trailer trash. Horrified, you hid behind a mask that portrayed you as sexy, desirable, and popular. Ten years later, feeling lost and alone, you begin the search for the real you. You're searching to find your real voice, your real passion, your true, authentic nature, but you refuse to take off the mask because you hate what you fear is behind it.

Maybe your shame is that you're selfish, rude, and therefore not as lovable as the other members of your family. So you cover it up with a mask that is nice, polite, and giving. You develop impeccable manners, great social skills, and a warm, welcoming smile. Then, one day when you can no longer stand the prison of your own polite and controlled environment, you seek to escape the confines of your facade, sensing that there is more to you than your mask will allow you to express. But when you try to break free from this fabricated self, your fear reins you back in because you don't want to feel the shame of being rude, selfish, and unlovable.

Maybe your shame is that you are a nothing and a nobody. In high school you decided to hide this fact by becoming a celebrated Overachiever. You joined the student council, made the honor roll, and even got into an Ivy League college. Twenty years later, no amount of achievement can bring the satisfaction you seek. The emptiness you feel drives you to start seeking more meaning and purpose. You begin to understand that there is more to you and your life than your achievements. But again, when you get close up, you start to feel the deep toxic shame of the past, when you felt like a nobody. So instead of going inside yourself and finding what you seek, you turn away, looking for a way to make your mask a little more palatable.

Once our facade is firmly in place, we begin to be used by the nature of the mask we have chosen. If we are the Good Girl, we will seek out opportunities where we can show up as being helpful, kind, and useful. If we are Victims, we will unknowingly put ourselves in precarious situations where we will be used, abused, and taken advantage of. If we are People Pleasers, we will find exactly those people to latch on to—usually people whose approval we crave—who will ask us to do things for them so we can say yes even when we are dying to say no. In other words, we attract to us the very people who will help us ensure that we can continue playing the same character over and over again—even when it has become so painful that we can no longer take it. We stay glued to our costumes because we believe we are the mask we are wearing. We have mistaken the person we are with the persona we've become.

Our personas often start off as a protective mechanism and soon become what imprisons us. They are the invisible cages that limit our full self-expression and rob us of our ability to be fully ourselves. It's like a game of hide-and-seek: we hide our undesirable qualities and then later need to seek them out in order to reclaim the authentic self beneath our masks.

Our social masks were not created randomly or by happenstance. They were constructed gradually, to cover the shame we felt as a result of incidents that left us feeling bad about who we are. As a coach and seminar leader specializing in emotional and spiritual education, I have spent the last twenty years teaching people from every walk of life to recognize their masks and begin to dismantle them. It is an astonishing and moving experience to bear witness to the magical unwinding of the fabricated self in a truly safe and supportive environment. We really know so much more about the modus operandi of our wounded egos than we think we do. At a recent intensive workshop for students participating in one of my advanced training programs, I asked everyone in the group to share the core shame they have carried throughout their lives and the mask they have worn to cover it.

The following vignettes offer a poignant glimpse inside the facades of essentially high-functioning, well-educated men and women just like you and me. Read them and you just may find threads of your own shame that you can begin to pull on and unravel. Imagine someone standing in front of the room, saying . . .

My shame is that I'm a dirty, flirtatious slut, and I cover this up by dressing conservatively, shutting down sexually, and keeping men at a distance.

My shame is that I'm a lesbian who doesn't belong. I cover this up by being funny, having lots of friends, and always being the life of the party.

My shame is that I am insensitive and uncaring. I cover it up by being charming, a great listener, and attentive to everyone's needs.

My shame is that I'm not good enough, smart enough, or pretty enough, and I cover it up by pretending to be perfect. I have the perfect kids, the perfect house, and the perfect job.

My shame is that I'm damaged—a loser. I cover it up by being a corporate trainer and motivational speaker.

My shame is that I'm weak, powerless, and dirty. I cover it up by looking everyone in the eyes and making them feel like a million dollars.

My shame is that I'm as insane as my alcoholic brother. I cover it up by being a financial powerhouse and keeping all my affairs in impeccable order.

My shame is that I'm scared to death of men. I cover it up by shamelessly exposing myself and wearing low-cut, sexy clothes and bright red lipstick.

My shame is that I have disdain for most people, and I cover it up by being an involved, caring leader in my community.

My shame is that I'm a coldhearted bitch, and I cover it up by being exceptionally warm, loving, and personable.

My shame is that I'm a pathological liar, and I cover it up by talking to everyone about the importance of honor and integrity.

My shame is that I live off my parents' wealth, and I cover it up by pretending to be successful and claiming to own a multi-million-dollar business.

My shame is that I'm an unwanted reject, and I cover it up by always being in a relationship.

My shame is that I'm a bigot, and I cover it up by befriending people of every race and color and inviting them into my home.

It is my hope that these examples will help you understand the mechanism that creates and shapes the false self. Although it took some time for the participants in my workshop to find the courage to be that transparent and vulnerable, the transformation that occurred for each of them following this process was life-changing, heart-opening, and well worth the inquiry.

PART TWO

THE PEACE TREATY

8

THE MASKS

In order to find peace, we must expose the masks we use to hide behind; the facades that we use to disguise our shame are oftentimes obvious to everyone but ourselves. Unbeknownst to us, the identity of our masks is usually tattooed across our foreheads. The masks we take on can be categorized without much effort, not only because there are just a few major wounds that we all share and collectively suffer from, but because as we move along in life we are always copying each other, mimicking others' behaviors, and adopting one of the "tried and true" disguises that we believe will take us where we want to go. If our wounds are around helplessness, powerlessness, abandonment, or betrayal, we might take on one of the masks of the victim. If our wounds are around domination, force, control, or abuse, we might take on one of the faces of the victimizer.

The masks we select for ourselves depend in large part on whether our natural tendency is toward being a victim or a victimizer—predator or prey. Inside the scientific theory of natural selection, the predator-prey relationship is central to nature's design, and it's also built into our human design. We see this dynamic at work with foxes and rabbits, leopards and zebras, cats and mice. It is a fascinating and paradoxical interdependence built right into our living systems. The food chain that we rely on for our survival remains unbroken for one simple reason: some of us are predators while others are prey. One type cannot exist without the other, and both are needed for balance and harmony. Understanding this aspect of our basic human nature not only gives us an important clue as to the masks we use to hide our shame, but also lays the groundwork for bringing ourselves back into balance and making peace with the opposing aspects of ourselves that have been at war.

The underlying message of the predator is: "I will feed upon you and destroy you. You are my victim." Predator types step over boundaries, seek control, and take what isn't theirs. They are forceful, aggressive, calculating, and manipulating and are looking out for their best interest at all times—even if they appear to be looking out for the interests of others. Predator types hardly take an action unless there is some payoff for themselves. They strive to get ahead, fulfill their needs, and "get theirs," regardless of who gets hurt in the process. On the other hand, the underlying message of the prey is: "I am powerless over you. Please don't hurt me. I can't help myself." While predators are focused almost exclusively on their own needs, prey types orient themselves around how they can please others, stay out of the way, or fit in better. Accommodating others is the primary way that prey types ensure their survival. Their strategy, whether they are aware of it or not, is to give others what they want, hoping that by doing so they will not get hurt. Prey types are passive, yielding, fearful, insecure, and therefore easily manipulated.

Look on any school-yard playground and you will find the kid who's hitting and the kid who's getting hit. If you are a parent who has two or more children, you may have noticed that one is more aggressive while the other is more passive. In any corporate office complex, you will find the person who is strategizing and manipulating those around them to get ahead, and you will find the person who is overburdened from picking up the slack of those who aren't getting their jobs done and taking the subtle abuse of a few office bullies.

The predator may show up as the man who pushes women too far sexually or the woman who uses her powers of seduction to gain entrance into the world of her choosing. Predators can be seen in every walk of life as those whose very nature is to dominate, exploit, and gain control over others. Of course, the natural counterpart and indispensable companion of the predator is their prey. The woman who hides beneath forty pounds of excess weight because subconsciously she believes herself to be sexually vulnerable is a prey type. The man who repeatedly works until ten at night to avoid the wrath of his boss and keep his job is a prey type. The dynamic that exists between the two is unfailing: predators can sniff out their prey from ten miles away, while prey types are inexorably drawn to predators like moths to a flame.

But here is where the plot thickens: prey and predator often camouflage themselves in order to be perceived as the other. We see this in the animal world, where more vulnerable creatures puff themselves up to look more fierce, while fierce hunters hide their claws and teeth to gain access to their prey.

I used to considered myself to be a predator—a "no one can mess with me; I can take care of myself" kind of woman. I even prided myself on helping vulnerable prey types by teaching them how to take care of themselves. And whenever anything bad happened around me, I would always take responsibility for it because I saw myself as a predator. Then one day, after having been betrayed, used, and lied to by a whole parade of people, I realized I was their perfect target. To turn the old fable around, I was the sheep in wolf's clothing! But for a good portion of my life, I would not acknowledge that I was prey. Because I felt so vulnerable as a child, I much preferred to see myself as a predator and would do anything to avoid the embarrassment of being seen as a weak victim who couldn't take care of herself. Ironically, my mother was always pointing out to me the ways people were taking advantage of me. "It's written all over your face," she would say. *"Easy target!"* I would get mad at her because I was so attached to being seen as strong. So even when I was warned (and I was!), I refused to protect myself. Finally, after too many incidents had proved me wrong, I had to admit that although I was disguised as a tough predator type, my basic nature is that of prey. This realization changed my life forever.

Thomas, an old client of mine, played the opposite game. In his personal life he was always cheating on his girlfriends and violating the trust of lovers and friends alike. Unconsciously, he was mortified by his behavior because it didn't fit with the picture he wanted to project in the world. He worked especially hard to counteract his predatory behavior in his professional life by being the nice guy, the reliable worker, and wrapping himself in a nonthreatening, almost boyish persona. But he couldn't suppress his true nature, and despite his best efforts to play by the rules, he found himself going after exactly what he wanted and conquering it—regardless of who stood in his way. While no one was looking, Thomas climbed to a very high-ranking position in his company. His "prey" mask was so expertly worn that nobody suspected his true potency, and they hardly realized he was taking over until he was already at the top.

Each of us has a basic nature—a proclivity toward being predator or prey—and it is out of this primary nature that our masks are created. Information is power here. If you are prey, you will never be able to protect and empower yourself unless you acknowledge this fact. If you're a predator who is victimizing and abusing others, you will only be able to alter your behavior if you are first willing to acknowledge that this is, in fact, your nature. In my own case, I didn't have the insight to spot the real predators because I was so busy pretending to *be* a predator and denying that I needed to be leery of others. Until I was willing to see myself as prey, I could never take care of myself and admit who the real predators were because in doing so I would have blown my own mask! The inquiry into your predator/prey nature is an edge-of-your-seat ride into the forces that have shaped the mask of your false self.

To get clear and discover your mask, you have to be willing to investigate your motives and your behaviors—to find out who you are underneath the face you show the world. The problem with this is that your wounded ego will lead you to believe that if you find out who you really are, you will hate yourself, which of course is the biggest lie there is. In my business, we call the ego a *trickster* because it is a master of disguise, always hiding itself from you—the one person who really needs to understand it. It is always dressing up, putting on its mask, slipping behind veils of denial, and pretending to be something it is not. So you have to be diligent and keenly aware in order to find it.

So again, we face another of life's paradoxes: For the ego to take its rightful place and return to its healthy function—as just one part of us—we must know all its moves and its motives. We must understand its design and recognize its flaws. We must be aware of its needs and its inadequacies, its gifts as well as its limitations. But the problem, of course, is that the function of the ego is to be a chameleon and to hide itself from itself, to be different, and to act in ways that will ensure its safety, ways that will guarantee it will not be destroyed. Survival is the ego's primary mission. To ensure that we are not going to sabotage ourselves or find ourselves in the midst of another's self-destruction, we must do the best we can to know when we are being true to our higher, more evolved self and when we have slipped back behind the mask of the wounded ego.

Of course, you can choose not to go on this scavenger hunt to unmask your false self. But if you want to see how you became the person you are today, why you behave the way you do, and why you attract the kinds of experiences you attract, I invite you to examine each of the following masks and rank them in the order in which you think they might apply to you. You should know that most of us wear at least two main masks—the one we show in public, and the one that reveals itself when no one else is around. Our public mask is almost always constructed to win us approval, admiration, love, acceptance, or attention while our private persona reveals more about the way we really feel about ourselves. In public, you might be the Savior, contributing and helping all those around you, while in private you are the Loner, isolated and in pain. In public, you might wear the mask of the Overachiever, while in your close private circle you don the mask of the Depressive. I want to challenge you to identify both your public mask and your private facade. Only then can you peel away the layers of denial that stand between you and the greatest expression of your authentic self.

As you engage in this inquiry, be aware that oftentimes the qualities we find most revolting in others are characteristics of our own masks. So as you read through these descriptions, be mindful of the people you have encountered throughout your life whom you have judged to be fake, phony, or inauthentic. In identifying their mask, you will become better able to see your own. Often we are horrified by the mask we wear, only we don't even know we are wearing it. So when we see it on another, we feel repulsed, judgmental, and, more often than not, hostile or upset. We're so busy trying to convince ourselves we are someone we're not that it's difficult for us to recognize the imposter we've become.

If you hate a particular mask, it is more than likely that either you wear the opposite mask (to prove that you are not that) or you are wearing that very mask and are unable to see it. As the Buddhist teaching reminds us, even if we have sight, there is still one person in the world we cannot see: ourselves. The only way we can see ourselves is in the reflection of another.

Recently, I was at a charity event when a girlfriend of mine came over and whispered in my ear, "I can't stand Melissa! She's so *phony*." When I looked over at Melissa, I noticed that she seemed to be wearing the mask of the Eternal Optimist—the overly gushy, fawning, happy type. It took me by surprise because my girlfriend is exactly like her. In fact, if I had put my girlfriend's face on Melissa and viewed her movements from afar, no one would have known I had made the switch. Like Melissa, my dear friend is a bit too loud, too overdone, and too exaggerated to be real.

The same thing occurred at dinner one night when a man I was dating came down hard on a character in a film we had just seen. The character was a charming Casanova type, and my date hated him and therefore the film and the director. In one fell swoop, he tore down a movie that was being nominated for an Oscar—while I sat there stunned because the behaviors he hated in the lead character were exactly like the moves he had made on me that won my heart.

Ultimately, the false self doesn't care what mask it uses as long as it does the trick and hides its hurt and shame. Its function is to protect us, to be the driver of our lives, and it believes it possesses the supreme force that will win us the big prize. Its song is: "I'm your vehicle, baby, and I'll take you anywhere you want to go."

By exploring the intricacies and subtleties of each of the faces of the false self and the masks of the wounded ego, and by understanding the shame and fear that gave birth to them, we can discover the spiritual solution that will ultimately lead to the healing and integration of our false self and our wounded ego.

The Masks of the Wounded Ego

THE SEDUCTRESS

The Seductress is after one thing and one thing only: to make herself feel better about who she is. Birthed out of the fear that she is not good enough, loved enough, and does not belong unless she is the object of someone's attention, she searches until she finds a suitable target to trap in her energetic web.

She's considered a predator because her main goal is to feed on the self-esteem of another in order to soothe her own emotional wounds. The Seductress literally throws out an energetic hook by being kind, loving, interested, and sexual—luring her next victim closer, all the while planning her next move. She spends her time thinking about how she looks and how others will perceive her. Her "catch," so to speak, enhances her inner perception of herself and covers, at least for the moment, the enormous pain and self-loathing that are stored in her psyche.

The real danger of the Seductress is that she doesn't know her motives, and her victims cannot see them. She doesn't care who she hurts or what costs her next victim will incur. Her motives and moves develop in time as she learns the insecurities and vulnerabilities of her prey. We would think her prey would be just men—often married (a bigger kill, so she thinks)—but they can be co-workers, a boss, other women, or anyone else in a position to serve her greater mission: to take others' light and use it to fill the dark hole of her own emptiness. Her prey of choice might be women if she prefers having women as sexual partners. In her private life, she will surround herself with those who are weaker than she is—but publicly she may pursue those who appear to be more powerful. *Dangerous, poisonous,* and *venomous* are the qualities I use to describe the Seductress, because her main attack is disguised in "love." Her signal broadcasts in all directions, sometimes loudly and at other times as a soft whisper: "I will give you some love if you give me your power. I am going to make you feel better about yourself if you give me some control. I am going to tell you everything you ever wanted to hear if you just make me the object of your attention."

The Seductress's Shame

Ordinary, undesirable, self-hating, unlovable,
empty, a nobody

The Seductress's Challenge

The Seductress's challenge is to recognize that her craving for the attention, admiration, and affection of others is a desperate cry from her inner world that she needs to give these things to herself. She must be willing to feel the emptiness and withdrawal pains that she will encounter when she is without an object to arouse, amuse, and seduce with her charms. Once she understands that what she seeks can be found only from within, she can set out on the healing journey of reconnecting with her higher self, which will fill her emotional void and enhance her self-esteem.

THE CHARMER

The Charmer is the charismatic lover who can melt even the toughest defense with a smile. Charmers are masters of manipulation, always using your weaknesses to win favor with you. They are adept at sizing people up and seeing who needs some love, some attention, or some hope, and then using this information as their weapon to open the door to your heart or pocketbook. Well-versed, well-educated, and often well-traveled, they can quickly become your best friend, a person to confide in and share your secrets with. But you want to be careful, because the Charmer is a predator. Before you know it, he is searching to see how he can get into your pants, your bank accounts, your business, or your heart. His sneakiness is one of his most deceptive qualities. Little did you know that the Charmer is keeping tabs on what you eat, where you shop, and what your favorite movies are so that he might use this data at a later time to show you how important and special you are. Charmers are great at seducing both men and women, and they get off on knowing how easy you are. Suave, cunning, and secretly hostile, they can literally charm you out of house and home. They are often great con men and never think twice about telling you a lie or twisting the truth—all in the name of trying to make you feel better about yourself.

The Charmer's Shame

Inferior, worthless, powerless, invisible, mediocre, unwanted

The Charmer's Challenge

The Charmer's challenge is to recognize that although he does have the charisma to take shortcuts in order to get what he wants, he will never feel good about himself as long as he is preying on another. The Charmer may need to look deeply into his own past—to the moment he decided that his best chance for success was to con people out of theirs. The path to wholeness for the Charmer is to recognize how bad he feels about himself, practice telling the truth, and cultivate feelings of self-worth by making powerful choices.

THE PEOPLE PLEASER

People Pleasers are one of my favorite types because, even though their behavior is rooted in sheer selfishness, they are actually good down to their core, and their need to please others usually helps someone else. True People Pleasers are generally people who were wounded badly in childhood—shamed until their needs no longer seemed important to them—and learned at a young age that to survive with the least amount of stress thrown at them, they should try with all their might to make others happy. People Pleasers are prey for the predator types and feel deeply ashamed that they are just not worth the space they take up in the world. Their feelings of worthlessness, and the fear that they are nothing without someone else's love or approval, leave them with a driving need to prove their worth to others. People Pleasers are the ones with a warm smile on their face and the word *prey* stamped on their forehead. They are driven to capture your love by doing, overdoing, and then doing some more. They will give until there is nothing left of themselves and covertly feed off the one they are giving to in a less than healthy way. They may take the form of the love buyer, buying gifts and spending money that they don't have, in order to gain love. Their food is the adoration of others, and although they may look like they are giving, they are actually taking.

People Pleasers are always seeking the validation of others for all that they do. Unfortunately, their deep feelings of inadequacy rob them of actually hearing how important and appreciated they are to their receiver. When People Pleasers are acting from their emotional wounds, their self-sabotage comes from their inability to hear what another might truly want from them.

Looking through their own filter of "How can I please you?" cuts them off from hearing, listening to, and being in touch with appropriate behavior, thereby cutting themselves off at the foot. The shadow of People Pleasers is their deep shame that they are nothing without you. "You" is whomever they happen to be attached to at the moment, together with the deeds they are doing on "your" behalf to prove how necessary they are.

The People Pleaser's Shame

Useless, forgettable, insignificant, disposable, needy, unwanted, passive aggressive

The People Pleaser's Challenge

The People Pleaser's challenge is to admit that they have been using the guise of giving as a way to feed their own sense of belonging and importance. By allowing themselves to feel the hidden emotions that they suppress through the act of giving, they begin to recognize how in need they are of their own charity. Once the People Pleaser surrenders to the fact that their job is not to please another, they can focus all of their attention and energy on the one person they do have the power to please: themselves.

THE BULLY

We all know the Bully when we see them. They are usually outwardly loud and pushy. They are the kid on the playground who is always taunting, finger-pointing, and pushing others around, and they are the adult in the boardroom who uses control, intimidation, and threats to get what they want. The Bully wants what they want when they want it, and they never think twice about pushing you around to get it. They dominate and control by force, and their secret weapon is your fear. Because they are inwardly driven by a deep fear of being dominated or controlled, they intuitively understand the depth of fearfulness that other humans possess. They have great instincts for survival, so they can easily spot the weak, and they prey on those whom they know will cower in fear or will lack the courage or the might to retaliate against them. Although they appear strong because they pick on those who are weaker than they are, at their core the Bully is insecure and suffers from deep feelings of inadequacy.

Bullies are cowards in disguise. Scared to death that they will never measure up, they try to compensate for their deep feelings of inadequacy by conquering others. They are to be feared because they are so deeply hurt and wounded that they will usually try anything to prove they are bigger, better, and more important than you. Their aggressive mask hides the fact that they are scared to death that you will find out who they are and expose their smallness.

The Bully's Shame

Weak, afraid, insecure, powerless, loser, coward

The Bully's Challenge

The Bully's challenge is to realize that although using force may win them the short-term battle, it will also win them many enemies along the way. By finding acceptance for their weakness, admitting when they feel powerless, and embracing their vulnerability, they actually place themselves in a position of authentic power.

THE QUIET SNAKE

The Quiet Snake is a trickster because you actually think they are harmless. Their quiet demeanor is disarming and even makes you feel sorry for the fact that they are so repressed. They are usually cordial but not overly friendly until they know that you are fair game for them. They may share information about their business deals or talents in an almost modest way, hinting around at opportunities that are available only for the lucky few. Their manner and manners make anyone who is nostalgic for the days of good, old-fashioned honor and respect an easy mark, and once they find their way into your life, they will figure out how to rob you of your ideas, your money, your social connections, and your dignity. Watch out, because their seeming innocence covers up a hoard of deceit. They often think of themselves as the smart one, but this sneaky, docile facade is just a smoke screen to hide that they are dependent, untalented, inadequate, and unable to make it on their own.

Quiet Snakes are predators who often disguise themselves as prey—the proverbial wolves in sheep's clothing. They are conniving, manipulating, cunning, and sneaky. They are often coy and will pretend to be more sensitive and vulnerable than they actually are in a ploy to win your trust. Slippery and hard to figure out, they hide behind a mask of innocence and work hard to make others feel safe, all the while calculating their next move. Their unconscious feelings of jealousy and worthlessness fuel

their desire to appear trustworthy and innocent, but beware—
they are not.

The Quiet Snake's Shame

Small, insignificant, powerless, not good enough, inadequate, con artist, liar

The Quiet Snake's Challenge

The Quiet Snake's challenge is to recognize that they are not so harmless. Because they may have convinced even themselves that they are quiet, innocent victims, the first and most difficult challenge of the Quiet Snake is to admit that they are, in fact, a predator. What the Quiet Snake needs to do is pay close attention to their inner dialog and realize their true intentions. Quiet Snakes need to catch themselves in the act of calculating their next move. Telling the truth will be the biggest challenge they face, because they are masters of deceit. Being straight about what they want forces the Quiet Snake out of hiding so they can discover their authentic power and their true worth.

TOO COOL

The person wearing the Too Cool mask goes to great lengths to convince you that everything's cool, they have no worries, and all is under control. "It's all good. What's the problem?" is their motto, and they are convinced there is no need to change because everything is exactly as it should be, even if the people around them are angry, upset, or falling apart. They appear indifferent, too busy with their own absorbing activities to be overly concerned with outside events, which earns them kudos from others who compliment them on how relaxed and easygoing they are.

Afraid of rocking the boat, these people project the image that they are confident in themselves and take everything in stride when in fact they are standing on very shaky ground. Beneath their calm exterior is the distressing belief that they are incapable of dealing with the scary unpredictability of other people and the world at large. Behind the mask of seemingly impenetrable composure is a feeling of great impotence in dealing with conflict or negativity. When confronted by an upset friend, family member, or an angry customer or client, they wear an easy smile on their face, unwilling to let others' problems penetrate the protective bliss of their emotional aloofness.

Too Cool types are actually liars who can easily deceive themselves and others about how they really feel. If they got in touch with their own dissatisfaction, hurt, anger, or other "heavy" emotions, they would open the door to others' dark sides, too. And the fear that all hell would break loose if they admitted the depth of their despair has them go on a chase for ways to numb their true feelings. They may choose a shopping spree, a drug, a yoga class, or a wave—anything to keep their deeper problems at bay.

Too Cool's Shame

Incapable, impotent, overly sensitive, out of control, wimp

Too Cool's Challenge

Too Cool's challenge is to get real and acknowledge and embrace the imperfect world. Because they are so driven by the need to appear perfect, those wearing this mask must challenge themselves to pay a little less attention to outer appearances and a little more attention to their inner experience. They must be willing to confront the terror they feel when they sense they are out of control and grant themselves permission not to have it all together. The Too Cool type will soon realize that the things they considered to be their biggest flaws actually make them more human, and therefore endear and connect them to those who love them.

THE MARTYR

Martyrs are always hard at work to save the world, sacrificing themselves in order to take care of everyone else. They hold the world on their shoulders because deep down they believe that everyone else is either incompetent or a full-blown idiot. Their heavy workload, whether it's saving the world or just their own family, causes them to feel superior to the rest of us because they are the self-pronounced heroes of the world. Because they sincerely believe that if they don't do a good job everything will fall apart, they force themselves to handle everything.

The Martyr's "holier-than-thou" role causes them to overstep boundaries and demand more than is humanly possible of the people around them. They have no use for the common person unless, of course, that person will join in and help their cause. They might be the kindest of the predator types, because they abuse their prey only when it serves the greater whole. Unfortunately, their nemesis is themselves, because no amount of doing will ease their guilt and shame at not doing or being enough. The Martyr is the self-proclaimed center of their own universe.

Because they are prone to becoming self-absorbed and single-minded in their mission, they often get sideswiped by those around them and end up feeling deeply hurt because, after all, they are doing so much and trying so hard. The Martyr has a justified excuse for manipulating others in the name of making the world—or just their home—a better place. Martyrs are know-it-alls and believe themselves to be above the rest of us incompetent people. Their need to be valued and valuable gives them a callousness that is well hidden.

The Martyr's Shame

Irresponsible, self-absorbed, out of control, powerless, disposable, useless

The Martyr's Challenge

The Martyr's challenge begins by accepting the fact that their motives are not as selfless or lofty as they lead others to believe. For every self-sacrificing deed, the wounded ego of the Martyr type receives a payoff—be it in the form of respect, admiration, or just a good, old-fashioned dose of pity from others. By recognizing the deeper need that is trying to get met through sacrificing themselves (which is to allow themselves to feel loved), Martyrs can adopt a more responsible stance, consciously choosing what they will do to care for others and what they will do to care for themselves.

THE GOOD GIRL

The Good Girl goes out of her way to let everybody know what a positive force she is in the world. Always bringing a ray of sunshine and a sweet smile with her, the Good Girl wants you to know that she is a nice, decent, prim and proper lady who always follows the rules. The first to ask how your children are doing in school or how your mother is getting along, the Good Girl oozes thoughtfulness, always the first to lend a supportive ear or a motivational pep talk to those in need. The Good Girl jumps at the opportunity to overlook her needs for the needs of another, because she believes that being good is the source of her worthiness. She is a plain Jane who knows how to mind her own business, and doesn't need to stand out. In fact, as a prey type, she's programmed not to stand out. You know her: she is the one who brings cookies and casseroles to all your events and charity functions and volunteers to clean up at the end. But she could just as easily be the one to carry on an affair with another woman's husband, while pretending to be her friend.

So committed is the Good Girl to upholding her image that she projects this mask onto her family, friends, and community as well. Often she flat-out refuses to see any slice of reality that could be construed as negative. She does not want to talk about conflicting urges, and she never cops to any feelings of jealousy, pettiness, or rage. Beneath her tidy facade, the Good Girl fears her own messy and unpredictable humanity and closes the door on anything that does not match her self-image.

The Good Girl's Shame

Imperfect, undesirable, broken, deceitful, bad

The Good Girl's Challenge

The Good Girl's challenge begins with acknowledging the experiences she had early on in life that led her to believe she is a bad girl and that to be loved, accepted, and belong she must project an image of goodness and perfection. By scratching beneath the surface of her Good Girl persona, she begins to expose her authentic yet rejected impulses and desires. Only when she is in touch with these can she recognize them as important and valuable aspects of her nature. This allows the Good Girl to get honest. Good Girl types often do not find the motivation to change until they have exhausted themselves by trying to prove how perfectly good they are or have suffocated themselves inside the confines of their masks. Once unmasked, the Good Girl can look forward to reclaiming her power and experiencing more genuine and fulfilling levels of self-expression.

THE NICE GUY

Lacking the backbone to ask for what he wants directly, the Nice Guy conceals his desires by putting on a facade that he is helping you. Friendly, empathic, supportive, and concerned, the Nice Guy believes that if he can make you happy, he will be happy, too. The Nice Guy is everybody's trusted friend, the kids' athletic coach, the community service leader. He may have even chosen a career as a teacher, insurance agent, minister, or practitioner of the healing arts, because he feels at home in settings where the attention is on others rather than on himself.

Somewhere along the line the Nice Guy decided that to be bold and direct meant trouble, especially with women, so he learned to keep his opinions and raw emotions to himself. As he gets up in years, he finds fewer and fewer places to stuff his feelings, which is why he is prone to passive-aggressive acts and rare but brutal fits of anger that are often out of proportion to the situation at hand.

When given a chance and nobody is looking, sometimes the Nice Guy will delight in doing things that are not so nice. Cutting other drivers off in traffic, giving bill collectors the slip, cursing his wife or children under his breath—even entertaining fantasies of destruction, terrorism, or adultery—give the Nice Guy a momentary bit of relief from the suppressing thickness of his facade.

The Nice Guy's Shame

Spineless, hurtful, selfish, bad boy, manipulative, vindictive

The Nice Guy's Challenge

The Nice Guy's challenge is to make peace with his mean, angry, and sometimes bad self. Because the Nice Guy has lived his life being a slave to other people's approval, his challenge begins when he decides to put his own preferences at the top of the list (not so nice). The next evolutionary step for every man who is wearing the Nice Guy mask is to become more overt with his requests and desires rather than sitting back and hoping they will magically be fulfilled if only he is nice enough. The ultimate challenge of the Nice Guy is to realize that it is not very nice to devote one's life to looking after others while failing to look out for oneself. Once the Nice Guy recognizes this pitfall, he can channel the energy he has focused on others into making his own needs a top priority and creating a life that's based in honesty and authentic power.

THE TOUGH GUY / TOUGH COOKIE

A hardened heart is the Tough Guy's or Tough Cookie's shield to protect the enraged child that lurks beneath the surface of their facade. They are too cool to care, too callous to connect from the heart. They are self-proclaimed predators who use the excuse that they have been beaten down by life, grew up too fast, or were robbed of their dignity when they were a child as a justification for their abrasiveness. If there was a sign tattooed across the face of the Tough Guy / Tough Cookie, it would read Don't Mess with Me. Unlike the Bully, the Tough Guy / Tough Cookie is not usually out looking to make other people feel bad (although often they do); they just want to be left alone and will mess with you only if they feel threatened by you or you get in their way.

These types are frequently in the principal's office, in the courthouse, or behind bars because they are too tough to care about the rules and thus they break them whenever they feel the need or the desire. If they are men, they pride themselves on being a "man's man," and if they are women, their femininity is well hidden behind an impenetrable leathery-tough exterior. They are driven by feelings of powerlessness and a deep sadness for how they—and their lives—have turned out. They were more than likely shamed early on for displaying their feelings or sensitivities and so now feel as though their survival depends upon the hardness of their shell.

The Tough Guy / Tough Cookie's Shame

Powerless, weak, needy, vulnerable, wimpy, a disappointment

The Tough Guy / Tough Cookie's Challenge

The Tough Guy / Tough Cookie's challenge is to discover what vulnerable, fragile feelings they are attempting to protect beneath their hardened facade. Although this mask serves to keep potentially hurtful people and experiences at bay, it also keeps love, success, and intimacy at a distance, which leads only to greater isolation. These types can channel their protective impulses in a much healthier direction by establishing good boundaries that protect their wounded hearts without blocking them from experiencing the full range of human emotions—including love.

THE ABUSER

Abusers are hurt and troubled individuals whose favorite pastime and extracurricular activities involve hurting other people. They are mean, vindictive, hateful, controlling, and manipulating—the scariest of the predator types. The nicest way to describe them is to say that they are deeply wounded—like a powerful animal that has been shot in the leg. Abusers are often psychological and emotional batterers. Always searching for their next victim so they can distract themselves from feeling the enormous amount of pain and self-hatred hidden in the deepest recesses of their psyche, they live for the feeling that they are better, stronger, and more powerful than someone else.

What makes the Abuser most dangerous is their ability to disguise themselves by wearing any combination of masks that hides their evil nature. They can be disguised as the public servant, the philanthropist, the religious leader, the dutiful son or husband, the grocery story clerk, or your local leasing agent.

The Abuser finds relief in taking their own self-hatred out on others, so they are always on the prowl for someone they can take advantage of, and no one is spared from their line of fire unless they serve a good purpose. If you have something the Abuser wants, watch out. They can twist a story better than anyone, ultimately convincing themselves and others that they are telling the truth.

In his book *People of the Lie,* M. Scott Peck notes that "one of the characteristics of evil is its desire to confuse." Abusers are adept at turning the tables, muddling the issues, and tricking their victims into believing that *you* are the one with the problem—or worse, that you were asking to be abused. They lie and then accuse you of being a liar. While all Abusers have conniving minds, some injure with their fists; for others, the weapon of choice is their tongues, their deceitful business techniques, or their absolute genius at manipulating the law and their prey. They believe the abuse they inflict on others is always the victim's fault, which makes it nearly impossible for the Abuser to ask for or receive help, even if it's mandated.

If you relate to the facade of the Abuser, or if you are in a relationship with one, I strongly recommend that you seek professional help.

The Abuser's Shame

Cowardly, wounded, powerless, deceitful, damaged goods

The Abuser's Challenge

The Abuser's challenge is to recognize the damage their actions inflict upon other people and the harm they bring—which is part of the problem, because they either are lacking a conscience (a defect in the human hard wiring) or have buried it long ago. In order to heal, they must realize that taking their rage out on others may relieve the internal pressure for a moment, but ultimately every act of abuse they perpetrate against another is an act of abuse they perpetrate against themselves. Their only hope for redemption is to find a power greater than themselves and to humbly ask that power for help. They must seek forgiveness from others and then themselves. They must find their own worth or they will never care about the harm they inflict on others. When the inner violence against themselves stops, the abuse against others will end as well.

THE ETERNAL OPTIMIST

The Eternal Optimist appears to be on a perpetual manic high. You always know when they walk into a room, because they are oversmiley, overzealous, and a little too eager to connect. The male version might give you a hug that is too close or lasts too long, and his ultrafriendly slap of hello may leave marks on your back. Gushing funny stories, telling jokes, and full of "pull my finger"-type pranks, he may overwhelm your children with his over-the-top exuberance.

You may have known a female Eternal Optimist in high school, because plenty of bouncy cheerleader types donned this mask. As an adult, this woman brings buckets of extra energy with her wherever she goes. Her voice is usually several pitches too high and several decibels too loud, and she may sound at least ten years younger than her chronological age. To the Eternal Optimist, being happy has become a competitive sport. Driven to prove that they are the happiest, friendliest, most loving person in the room, Eternal Optimists steal the show and hijack every conversation with their exaggerated responses. Whatever most people express, they express it a hundred times more. If something is good, it's "the best." If they are expressing gratitude, they can't thank you enough. Fearing that they are unlovable, they force themselves to put on a happy face and be the life of the party. For these types, being "nice" isn't good enough. They have to win you over with their performance. Having fun is the number-one commitment of the Eternal Optimist.

The trained eye can sometimes detect the edges on the Eternal Optimist's mask beginning to peel, the trained ear a tinge of stress in their forced laugh. To those who can see through their facade, Eternal Optimists seem phony and obnoxious. Others may find it exhausting to be around them.

Even when talking about sad things the Eternal Optimist may be smiling. The amount of happiness they feel compelled to express is proportionate to the amount of sadness they are concealing. They are terrified that if they allow even a bit of negativity to enter their minds, it will bring them down.

The Eternal Optimist's Shame

Sad, resigned, pessimistic, hopeless, rejected, desperate, unlovable

The Eternal Optimist's Challenge

The Eternal Optimist's challenge is to accept that life is just not a bowl of cherries all the time. The mask of the Eternal Optimist is a tough one to crack, because many hold being manically happy all the time as the gold medal in life. These types often argue the most fiercely that they are not wearing a mask at all. To support the Eternal Optimist in seeing through their own facade, I ask them to spend ten minutes a day looking in the mirror while doing their best "I'm so happy" routine. That's about all it takes for them to recognize the thin veil that separates their true self from their false persona. Ultimately, the Eternal Optimist's challenge is to be who they are without any sugar coating and to know deep in their hearts that they will be loved, accepted, and belong just as they are. They need to get quiet enough to feel the pain, embarrassment, or discomfort they are masking with their false exuberance and to give themselves permission to find out who they really are.

THE INTELLECT

Knowledge and information are both the currency and the weaponry of the Intellect. This mask is created out of an early experience that has left its victim with a belief that they are stupid, unimportant, and somehow not good enough. Emotionally crippled and afraid of painful feelings, wearers of this mask protect themselves behind thick layers of superiority and self-righteousness. Though they may or may not be well educated in a formal sense, the Intellect is blessed with a quick mind and great capacity to process and digest information. They use these mental gifts to effectively manipulate and hold themselves above others, often treating their peers in ways that are overtly or covertly condescending, belittling, and dismissive. This behavior may show up through their continually correcting friends, family, or co-workers. Even if the Intellect is not doing these things aloud or to one's face, you can be sure they are doing so within their internal dialog, noting stupidity and keeping an accurate tally of others' errors and shortcomings. They are the righteous know-it-alls, all dressed up in intellectual arrogance.

Living primarily in their heads, Intellects like to consider themselves as being above the messiness of emotions. They prefer to remain cool and detached, relying on logic rather than feeling to guide their decisions and actions. They will rarely allow themselves to become engaged in emotional situations or to stoop to the level of losing their cool. Instead, the Intellect prefers to engage in so-called discussions that emphasize the rationality and correctness of their own views while judging the other person to be wrong for being emotional and irrational. There is no way for others to win in these discussions, as the Intellect is always sure, always right, and always beyond challenge. This person is clever in the art of interpreting events in their own favor and is a master of spin, so even if they are proved wrong, they will masterfully contrive a viewpoint or framework for the situation that will ultimately prove them to be right after all.

Don't expect to get too close to wearers of this mask. Inside relationships the Intellect is prone to holding their partners at arm's length—at least emotionally. Unable to understand and effectively deal with feelings (their own and others), they show up as uninterested and aloof. At times they can demonstrate caring, concern, and even compassion as long as they are in control and feel safe. They can even express and profess to feel love, although it's usually based on some set of mental constructs rather than a true emotional connection with another. But threaten to crack the smooth and highly polished veneer of the Intellect and they will quickly retreat behind an impenetrable fortress of mental logic. Once they have made up their minds about something, they are difficult—if not impossible—to sway. Their biggest fear is that behind all their intellectual posturing, they will be discovered to be just another one of the idiots in the world.

The Intellect's Shame

Not good enough, less than, fearful, emotionally challenged, stupid, idiot

The Intellect's Challenge

Ultimately, the challenge for the Intellect is to give up reliance on the safe, neat, and rigidly structured stronghold of the rational mind and allow themselves to venture into the unpredictable, messy, risky, and oftentimes scary world of emotions and the heart. They must come to understand that knowing is often the booby prize and that true intimacy and emotional connection can be developed only when we balance the mind with the heart. By stepping out of their mental fortress and opening up to the ideas and feelings of others, wearers of this mask can begin to develop true compassion and intimacy.

THE SAVIOR

The Savior is the classic codependent caregiver, a rescuer who needs to be needed at all costs. Desperate to make your life better, these types are convinced that they know how to do it and know what's best for you. *If you would only listen to me!* is their main complaint and overall frustration. They are the first to jump in with advice, remedies, and answers to life's complexities, and they pride themselves on being resourceful, loving, and caring. The Savior is always in need of someone to fix, to comfort, and to help, because giving to others is the main way they ensure that they get something for themselves. Although they appear selfless, their motives are almost entirely selfish.

The mask of the Savior was most likely created as a way to deal with the dysfunction in their household—be it some form of abuse, family illness, or crisis. The person who adopted this mask found an escape from their own pain by "rising above it"— taking charge of everything and everyone, and working overtime to make it all better. By taking on this role and learning how to "be there" for others, they found a safe identity and also discovered a way to keep from feeling the depth of their own pain, hurt, and neglect. Professionally, this codependent caregiver might be driven to become a nurse, therapist, doctor, or teacher, because such occupations allow them to fulfill their reason and purpose for living—to help out some unfortunate soul.

The Savior is drawn to the addict, alcoholic, and victim—as they have an insatiable need to feel useful. However, on closer examination, this person often is a predator in disguise because they feed off the very people whom they profess to be helping.

They derive a sense of self-importance by caring for others and cleaning up the mess of other people's lives and will continue to take responsibility for those around them even if it costs them all their time, energy, and money. The Savior believes that in order to be loved they have to sacrifice their own needs for someone in greater need.

A sure way to spot the mask of the Savior is to ask them about their own lives. Almost exclusively, they will define themselves in relation to those whom they care for. They live vicariously through other people, tending to other people's lives but having no inner life of their own. Their self-sacrificing nature is lived out through being dedicated to a cause for which they are fighting—their job, their family, a spouse or loved one.

The Savior's Shame

Needy, useless, desperate, uncaring, selfish, less than

The Savior's Challenge

The Savior's challenge is to realize they get their identity by what they give and what they do, and that they are trying to get their needs met through this role. Saviors thrive on crisis, drama, and high stress—any situation in which they can show up as a rescuer—and as a result they often find themselves managing one bad situation or breakdown after another while neglecting their own needs. This makes them resentful and bitter, because they never feel appreciated, cared for, or compensated enough after all that they give. Their ultimate challenge is to admit that they give to get and that they are not the victims of those they are caring for. When they can take responsibility for their own unhappiness and find their own inherent worth, they will be free to have healthy relationships, set good boundaries, and live a life they are proud of.

THE DEPRESSIVE

The Depressive is the sad sack of the bunch, and gloom and doom are their constant companions. Always looking for what's wrong with themselves and their lives, they are masters at internalizing and holding on to their toxic emotions. Their deep disappointment and unprocessed anger at the outer world and those who occupy it are the culprits that destroy their spirits and wash away their dreams. Without realizing it, they cling to a past that has betrayed them, and in the process they avert anything good that may be trying to come their way. Scared of the future and overwhelmed by the fear that they will be unable to handle it, they unconsciously choose to hold on to the pain they know rather than chance what unknown pain might come to them should they open up to something new. In other words, the devil they know is better than the devil they don't know.

Depressives are addicted to misery—their own brand of negative internal ranting (which sounds something like *What's wrong with me? Why me? Poor me. It shouldn't have happened to me. Why don't I ever get mine?*)—and this leaves them in a vicious cycle of pain and hopelessness.

Depressives set themselves up to be preyed upon by others because they have quashed their true nature along with their God-given instincts and traded them for a hopeless, catastrophic fantasy that has a miserable ending. Wounded, scared, and without the resources to help themselves at an early enough stage, they begin the painful process of rejection and repression. You can always spot a Depressive because they wear a long face, their smiles are minimal, and the flame of their inner spirit is a dim flicker. Because they do not believe that new beginnings or exciting possibilities exist for them, it is difficult for them to let go of the past and move on. Somewhere along the line they sold their souls to be liked, to be loved, to be included, or to belong, and it didn't pay off. In fact, they were more than likely rejected, shunned, abused, or betrayed. How depressing is that? In their minds, life has turned against them and God either doesn't exist or has abandoned them. Their painful emotions were too much for them to digest or handle, so they did the only thing they knew how to do: they suppressed them, hid them, and withdrew from the world.

The Depressive is just that—depressing—because they are unable to see anything other than the small, dark world they have created for themselves. The possibilities that exist for their future are blurred by their inability to see what awaits them outside the confines of the grim story they are living within. Feeling desperate and alone, they crawl inside their wounds and painfully and hopelessly go through life just hoping to survive.

The Depressive's Shame

Hopeless, hurt, rejected, abandoned, unfixable, helpless

The Depressive's Challenge

The Depressive's challenge is to recognize the repetitive, negative loop they are listening to hour after hour, day after day, and stop it. They must fearlessly go into their painful emotions and give themselves permission to safely express the volcanic, negative, toxic energy that lurks beneath the surface of their depression, causing them to experience the aftershock sometimes years after an emotional trauma. By giving themselves permission to release their pent-up emotions, the Depressive can once again experience the full range of their feelings, forgive and move on. They must work hard to surround themselves with positive people and create a new vision for their lives. Working with those less fortunate may be their ticket to freedom.

THE JOKESTER

The Jokester is the first to make light of a serious, sad, or uneasy situation. Though they may be blessed with a genuinely good sense of humor, those wearing this mask have learned to use comedy as a defense mechanism, and now it is a knee-jerk response over which they have little conscious control. Deeply uncomfortable with their own sensitivity, and terrified that intimacy will inevitably lead to rejection, Jokesters are driven to say or do almost anything to diffuse the realness of the moment. Because they're unable to embrace the ambiguity of their own emotions, they have little capacity to establish a real connection with others. Their interactions are almost always aimed at advancing their agenda and trying to get others to love them and to see them as easygoing and personable in order to conceal how deeply uncomfortable they are.

If at times their humor appears tactless, it's because they are often oblivious to their surroundings and unconscious of the mood of those around them. Because they are so focused on getting a laugh, they lose the ability to discern whether their behavior is appropriate to the situation. When they have succeeded at evoking a reaction—even a negative reaction—from the crowd, the Jokester is momentarily reassured that they are in control and therefore safe. The social mask of the Jokester may have developed out of their relationship with an exceedingly critical, serious, or strict parent, when as a young child they discovered that being funny was a way to secure love and gain attention.

Despite a happy-go-lucky facade, the Jokester is actually very sad underneath the mask. The Jokester is continually working to win the love, acceptance, and friendship of those around them. Though they appear to be happy and well adjusted, they often come off as painfully inappropriate. The real tragedy is that even when the Jokester succeeds in winning people over, they never feel seen or appreciated for who they are beneath the mask. We've all heard the stories about the tragic lives of some of the funniest people in history. At best, the Jokester is a performer and is always left wondering whether people will actually love them when they stop putting on a show.

The Jokester's Shame

Unlovable, boring, worthless, different, reject, nothing special, inauthentic

The Jokester's Challenge

The Jokester's challenge is to first realize that their mask isn't actually securing them the love they seek, and that their deeper need for authentic connection will remain unmet for as long as their mask is in control. They need to develop the trust to know that they are enough—that they are lovable whether or not they are being funny or entertaining. Their challenge is to focus more on listening than on speaking in order to allow their appropriate and authentic self-expression to emerge. Above all, the Jokester must find acceptance for the full range of emotions that reside inside them; otherwise, the resistance and disdain they feel toward their own humanity will push them back into hiding. They must search and find their inherent worth outside of their humor.

THE ENTITLED SUPPORTER

The Entitled Supporter craves a high-profile lifestyle but lacks either the talent or the charisma to create it on their own. So instead they position themselves in proximity to someone who is loved by many and vicariously enjoy that person's popularity, fame, or notoriety. The Entitled Supporter can often be found in high-level support positions such as the personal assistant, the entourage member, the protégé, the prized student, the devoted disciple, the rock star groupie, the political handler, or the ever-present mother of the child prodigy. These people are irresistibly drawn to the limelight of another, and while they get their foot in the door by taking on a supportive role, what they really want is to be cast in the lead. The Entitled Supporter is a predator who feeds on other people's success.

The Entitled Supporter not only wants to share in their host's limelight; they want to steal it for themselves. Identity theft is their secret desire. Consciously or unconsciously the Entitled Supporter begins to emulate the person they admire, taking on the beliefs, the behaviors, and even the mannerisms or personal style of the person they consider to be their power source. They might be found snooping in the person's office when they're out, making friends with their friends, or exchanging contact information with business associates in hopes that they will soon be discovered for the star that they are and rewarded accordingly. They start out with a loving and supportive manner, but the jealousy of their wounded ego drives them to overstep the boundaries of a healthy friendship or working relationship. Convinced that they will lose power, status, or opportunities without the continued endorsement of their host, the Entitled Supporter works hard to ensure that they become an irreplaceable part of that person's life.

The Entitled Supporter works diligently and cheerfully when in the presence of someone they regard as having a higher social status than their own, but they can become rude or condescending to those they regard in one-down positions. In fact, the two-faced nature of this facade is its clearest hallmark. Most rock stars, actors, politicians, and successful CEOs have a trail of these people following behind them—riding in their wake, basking in their accomplishments, and quietly claiming them as their own.

The Entitled Supporter's Shame

Good for nothing, less than, second best, untalented, insecure, not special enough, sneaky

The Entitled Supporter's Challenge

The Entitled Supporter's challenge is to step out of the shadow of the person they have been supporting and establish themselves in their own right. To do so, they must acknowledge the ways they have been feeding on the energy of another while claiming it as their own. The Entitled Supporter must ultimately risk the security of their position with someone of fame in order to find their own authentic power. They must acknowledge that their role as a supporter is as important as the one they are serving. Humility must be practiced if they want to heal the deep wound that tells them that who they are is just not good enough. When the Entitled Supporter finds respect for themselves, others will respect them as well.

THE LONER

Scared to death of the human race, those wearing the mask of the Loner frequently withdraw into the cold isolation of their own inner world as a way of protecting themselves from dealing with their emotional issues and hidden pain. Rather than being an active participant in their lives, they retreat to the feel-good moments that they find through plugging in to work, a soap opera, a computer game, or the refrigerator. Whether they acknowledge it or not, their loneliness makes them vulnerable to addictive obsessions that relieve—at least for the moment—the deep pain of feeling that they don't belong, that they'll never be a part of something greater, and that they are on the outside looking in.

Loners are driven by the fear that they are inherently flawed, unwanted, not good enough, and that they serve no important purpose. Somewhere along the line the Loner decided that if they don't play, if they don't put both feet in, they will spare themselves from feeling the searing pain of trying to fit in and being left out. Loners are many times obese, in poor health, in debt, abusing alcohol or drugs, or addicted to shopping, gambling, or their vibrators. They are prone to using fantasy to keep themselves in denial about how desperate they are for real connections.

The Loner is the one who hangs back on the fringe, always on the outskirts, both at work and in their personal lives. They may try to trick themselves and others into believing that they are involved and connected—either by making the occasional cameo appearance or by positioning themselves in the proximity of someone who is well-connected. Either way, the Loner will always leave the back door open for a quick escape back into their private world where they feel they are alone and safe.

The Loner may put on airs, trying to pretend that the reason they choose solitude is that they are better than, smarter than, or more evolved than those around them. But this is nothing more than a rationalization and a lie that keeps them looking out at the world rather than being a part of it.

The Loner's Shame

Inherently flawed, sick, wounded, terrified, outcast, unlovable, alone

The Loner's Challenge

The Loner's challenge is to begin by admitting that they are, in fact, all alone. The mask they constructed to spare them from feeling lonely has actually driven them deeper into seclusion and shame. They must find the humility to acknowledge that they are no better or worse than anyone else, and they must be vulnerable enough to reach out and be seen, even though they feel imperfect. As they deal with the addictions that have kept them alone and ashamed, they become better able to ignore the voice that warns them that it's safer to retreat than to belong. Twelve-Step groups, a church, or a spiritual community can provide the Loner with the opportunity to let down their barriers and belong. Once they are connected to something larger than themselves and discover that they hold special gifts and their life matters, they no longer feel a reason to hide.

THE VICTIM

The Victim is the poster child for "Woe is me." "I can't believe that happened to me again" is their mantra. They have chosen the painful path of the powerless prey unable to get out of the way of abuse—whether it originates from others or from themselves. They can sniff out a bad situation and then, instead of avoiding it, walk right into it to ensure they can wear their crown of victimhood for yet another span of time. The Victim can rarely see how they participate in the creation of what you or I might consider unfortunate circumstances. Being wounded at a young age—and more often than not severely victimized by someone they loved—they sealed their fate with the disheartening and life-draining belief that they are helpless and powerless and that life is a painful place.

The attention they seek from being victimized becomes their underlying commitment. Not feeling worthy of being loved for anything besides the pity they conjure up from being victimized, they are in a constant state of chaos and feel helpless to do anything about their bad luck. Pity is something they both love and abhor. They love it because it gives them the much-needed attention they won't give themselves, and they abhor it because they live in a constant state of stress and anxiety over the adverse circumstances that seem to follow them everywhere. And just in case you're thinking that they are all limping around looking frumpy, wounded, and beaten down, you should know that the Victim is sometimes disguised as a high-functioning, successful person who appears to have it all; however, the quiet aching inside them robs them of the joy of their successes. "Poor me" is the stamp that every Victim wears across their forehead.

The Victim's Shame

Unlovable, unworthy of happiness, helpless, sad, powerless, resigned

The Victim's Challenge

The Victim's challenge is to take responsibility for the ways in which they have participated—consciously or unconsciously—in the unfortunate events of their lives. By claiming ownership of what they do have control over, they begin to see themselves as the designer of their own destiny. To penetrate the mask of victimhood, the Victim needs to be honest about what they get out of wearing this crown and then decide for themselves that the payoff is no longer worth the cost.

THE OVERACHIEVER

The Overachiever is the most driven person of the bunch. Although they are generally successful, they are also continuously busy, overwhelmed, and almost always overcommitted. They pride themselves on how many projects they can handle at one time and how many boards and committees they can participate in. They are the champions of the multitaskers. No matter how much they do, it is rarely enough to satisfy their insatiable hunger for success—which for them is food for their underappreciated wounded egos. Their feelings of unworthiness drive them to win at all costs, even if it means barreling over someone else. Achievements in the outer world are the yardstick by which they measure their inner worth.

Overachievers generally suffer from self-importance and egomania—a sure sign of their predatory nature. They are result-driven doers who won't take no for an answer—from themselves or others. They are perfectionists whose disdain for mediocrity has them micromanage every detail and become overly controlling. Unfortunately for those who fly with them, the Overachiever is often harsh, critical, impatient, and judgmental of all the regular folk who gather around them to feed off their success. Few can withstand their high energy, and fewer still can keep up with the Overachiever's frantic pace.

Overachievers feel entitled to better service, better lifestyles, and better benefits from those whose businesses they patronize, and as a result they often have unrealistic expectations and a hard time understanding the lifestyles of common, everyday people.

Inwardly unfulfilled and insecure, these types find it hard to sit still for even a moment. At their best, they are creative geniuses with enormous vision. At their worst, they are power-hungry people who seek the next big win at any cost.

The Overachiever's Shame

Worthless, less than, boring, average, useless, frightened

The Overachiever's Challenge

The Overachiever's challenge is to stop defining who they are by the measurement of what they do. When the Overachiever begins to place more value on their quality of life than they do their achievements, they learn to stop and savor the fruits of their labors rather than insatiably going after more and more. As soon as the Overachiever realizes that doing more is not an inoculation against being average, he or she is free to experience the moment—not as a measure of their value but as an opportunity to experience and enjoy life. They must find their inherent worth in just being who they are, without any of their ornaments of achievement.

Unmasking Your Authentic Self

Are you starting to see it? As long as you insist on keeping yourself crammed into an outdated, tight costume that you designed for your tenth, eighteenth, or twenty-first birthday, you will have to spend money you don't have, get in relationships that will break your heart, emotionally torture your kids into submission, listen to your demoralizing internal dialogue, falsify your résumé, cheat on your expense reports, have sex with people you don't know or don't love, deceive the people who love you, push around those weaker than you, and puff up your feathers and pretend to be someone you are not. As long as you can't admit to your flaws, weaknesses, hurts, and prejudices, you will have to blurt out racial slurs, gamble your money away, destroy your career, shake down your partners, blow up business deals, and enable those around you who are doing bad things.

If you insist on living as a small expression of your eternal self, you will have to work harder and harder to cover up all the feelings that are inconsistent with the facade you have chosen. You'll have to smile when you don't feel like smiling, do things you hate to do, keep your mouth shut when you feel like speaking up, pretend you're nice when you know you're not, buy people's love to keep them close, get suckered into bad deals to prove you are stupid, get extra degrees to prove you're smart, wear clothes that are too tight to get some attention, talk to people who bore you to convince others that you care, cheat people to convince yourself that you are successful, pretend that you are good and honest even when you are a con, work in jobs you hate with people you can't stand, indulge in addictions that destroy your spirit, traumatize those around you, and suffer the pain of being your own worst enemy

So you are now at the point where you must choose which path you are going to take. Are you going to take off the mask you've been wearing? Or are you just going to fix it up, put some lipstick on it, inject it with a bit of hope, or adorn it with some new clothes—in other words, fluff it up? Or will you choose to diligently and methodically dismantle that which is keeping you from experiencing the full expression of both your human-ity and your divinity? Most of us are just working to make our masks fit a little better, thinking that if we get a new hairstyle, a new job, a new lover, or more money we will feel better. But we're still just trying to feel better about a mask!

To step out of the masks we've been wearing for years and step into the greatest expression of our authentic self, we must be willing to expose the shame and fear that have served as the foundational slab of the face we show the world. We must be willing to identify our shame and fear for what they are: shame and fear that have turned against ourselves. We must give up trying to satisfy the insatiable hunger of the wounded ego and open the door to unexplored realms of reality that we may have ignored or shut ourselves off from years ago.

Discovering that we are not who we have believed ourselves to be is a difficult realization that only the courageous will make. What usually precipitates the discovery of our false self is, more often than not, a brutal attack from the outside world. Someone turns on us, lies to us, or betrays us. Someone steals our ideas, takes advantage of our good nature, or takes what is ours out of greed or jealousy. Maybe the outer event is caused by our own submissiveness, our own hunger for more, or our own thirst for power or prestige. Maybe our bodies turn on us, leaving us powerless to keep up the facade of our false personas.

To transcend the false self, heal the wounded ego, and ultimately become an integrated being, we must break through the web of lies that birthed our false selves and separate ourselves from the mask we've constructed in order to fit in, belong, and be loved. Once we are able to identify the beliefs that constructed it, we will see that our mask is just part of our wounded ego's story. Then, having seen behind the facade of our own mask, we begin to recognize the masks that other people wear as well. Only with this ability can we protect ourselves and keep ourselves from walking in harm's way.

My friend Jorge once told me about an ancient African religion that advocates hanging a mask in a visible location near the entrance of one's home. This custom serves as a reminder that people enter our lives under a variety of pretenses. It is believed that the symbol of the mask helps us to recognize and protect ourselves against those who are there to take rather than to give, or who may not have genuine friendship or our best interest in their hearts. Hanging a mask near the entranceway of our home reminds us to look past the outer facade of all who enter our lives and see the true nature of the person hiding behind the mask.

But we must also beware of our hidden motives and the mask we have created to hide behind. There is nothing easy about dealing with the deeper truth that we are living as a false expression of a greater, broader self. But indeed, the gifts that come with breaking free from the bonds of the restricted and tightly held-together false self are well worth the discomfort that we must go through as we peel away the layers of lies, distortions, false assumptions, and denial that hold together the mask of our self-made personas. The challenge and the opportunity is for us to wake ourselves from the trance of the false self that prevents us from experiencing the limitlessness of our true and authentic expression.

9

WAKING UP FROM DENIAL

To crack the code of the false self and penetrate the mask you've worn day after day and year after year, you must wake up from the trance of denial. Having the courage to break free from the denial of your wounded ego and be straight with yourself gives you the ability to acknowledge your shameful feelings, weaknesses, and flaws, as well as bask in your strengths and gifts.

Although most of us have heard the joke about denial being a river in Egypt, denial is no joke. It is a mechanism of our egos that can literally strip us of our dignity and our ability to create a life we love. Pain is the catalyst that triggers denial. When the collective wounds of our past become too great for our human heart to bear, an internal switch flips on that sends us into denial. It is no different than the hibernate function on a computer: the computer is still on, but it is operating in an energy-saving mode.

In the same way, going into denial temporarily conserves our resources as it numbs us, keeping us from feeling and having to deal with the painful emotions that lie beneath our denial. Denial is like a thin film, a layer of consciousness that suppresses our painful thoughts and feelings and allows us to look through a particular lens that can't or won't let us see the entire picture. Like the blinders we put on racehorses so they won't be disturbed by outside events, denial blinds us to what is really going on both inside and outside ourselves. When we are in denial we do just that: we deny—deny what is going on around us, deny the reality of the situation, deny our instincts and thoughts about a situation, deny our feelings, and deny the consequences of our actions and our nonactions.

Denial is a brilliant function within the human psyche. Each of us was designed with this built-in feature that protects us from experiencing the darkest, deepest recesses of our inner pain. When we are on the brink of overload, when our pain is so great that it threatens our emotional and psychological health, this defense mechanism of our ego structure is automatically activated. When the pain is more then we can handle, when we have no tools to deal with the trauma of a particular situation, we automatically kick in to the denial mode. There is nothing we can do to remove this switch, nor would we want to; it is built into our human hard drive for a very good reason: it is there to protect us. When we realize we have been blindsided, lied to, used, taken advantage of, conned, cheated, or misled— or that we have unconsciously done these things to another— our deepest shame and our most painful emotions get unleashed. For some of us, these feelings are so horribly painful that the only way we can deal with them is to go into a state of

146

denial. We resist accepting the truth of our situation because the pain of admitting it is far too great in the moment. We deny the outer reality in hopes that in doing so we can somehow make it turn out different than it is. We fluctuate between the pain-filled moments when the truth of our situation filters in and the fantasy-filled moments that are fueled by our denial. Even if we know that to stay in denial will only prolong the drama, trauma, and pain, the moments of solace we are able to find in the denial state seem worth the price. Our denial acts as a shield, protecting us from the devastation that we are not yet able to process.

In its highest function, denial serves us by protecting us from pain. Yet to our great detriment, it also blinds us from seeing our own destructive nature, which inevitably causes us more pain. It's another of life's great paradoxes. On one hand denial provides us with a temporary shelter from our heartache and helps us to cope with horrific circumstances, and on the other hand it blinds us to our self-destructive behaviors. Healthy denial helped millions of Jews in Nazi Germany endure the unimaginable terror of their day-to-day lives. In fact, when it failed to buffer people from the atrocities that were going on all around them, many chose to kill themselves rather than endure the torment any longer. A child being molested, a mother seeing her child get sick and die, a man losing his job in the middle of an economic depression, a woman being cheated on by the man she has given her heart to, someone being diagnosed with a deadly disease, a man losing his wife after fifty years of marriage, having your city bombed or blown away by a hurricane—all these situations and others of this magnitude would likely trigger the healthy denial needed to endure a devastating experience.

Although denial often persuades us to stay in bad situations, it also gives us an opportunity to adjust to painful and unwanted realities that we can't or don't believe we can escape from. When we are in the midst of someone doing something bad to us, denial becomes our primary survival mechanism. By concealing the depth of our pain, it offers us hope that things will get better. But to steer clear of its potentially destructive effects, we have to recognize that when our denial mechanism is triggered, it is a sign of distress, an emergency warning signaling trouble—no different than a fire alarm. Our internal system is sending out a message that there is trouble here and we need some assistance.

The Devastation of Denial

As healthy denial can assist us and protect us, unhealthy denial leads us to becoming our own worst enemy. Unhealthy denial is activated when we use it as an easy way out, when we are unwilling to face a particular truth about what's happening around us or what is happening to us. Denial kicks in when reality would require us to make an uncomfortable change in our lives that we don't want to make. This is how we are designed, for better (when denial saves us from feeling the full impact of a horrific circumstance like our husband or wife leaving us for our best friend) or for worse (when denial prevents us from confronting our online gambling habit and ten years later we find ourselves broke, in debt, and losing our marriage). I see it every day. How many people knew years before a blowup that they should deal with their issues of cheating, gambling, sex, drugs, or alcohol addiction, or with their child's behavior problems? In most cases, denial arrives as a good friend and ends up as an enemy. Let me explain.

By the time Lynn discovered she was with someone who was living a double life, she was already deeply in love with him. He had romanced her, wooed her family and friends, infiltrated her business affairs, and become an integral part of her life. Lynn was a successful businesswoman who was, at the time, in the middle of several big projects that seemed overwhelming to her. Every day was like a crash course in survival rather a wondrous journey through the magical life she believed she had created. Her fear that she would not be able to juggle all the balls she had in the air caused her to go into denial about what was happening in her personal life. She desperately wanted to believe that her made-up reality was the truth, so when anything that was inconsistent with that reality showed up, she would quickly hide, justify, or dismiss it—the three actions of denial.

As is always the case, the moment Lynn sidestepped her intuition and looked the other way, she could no longer trust herself. By betraying her own instincts, she skewed her ability to see clearly, sending her further and further into denial about what was really happening in her own home. Ten years later, after turning her finances over to the man who was now her husband, she discovered that he was not, in fact, who he said he was. Denial may have saved her some heartache in the moment, but the bill came later, when she discovered that all her bank accounts had been wiped out.

Once we turn our heads and no longer acknowledge the truth that is staring us in the face, we can no longer distinguish between the reality of our present circumstances and what we want to believe to be the truth. Our minds can no longer see which is correct. Our psyches will usually opt for the reality that is easiest to endure emotionally. Our denial kicks into action, overriding both our instincts and our better judgment. The painful emotions that emerge as we begin to come to terms with the reality of our situation show up as unwanted intruders. And like most good humans, we will do anything to avoid feeling the dark cesspool of negative emotions that lie dormant within each of us.

Most of us are not just in denial about our present circumstances but also deny some aspect of our past. We might deny the severity of our childhood experiences—blocking out what we didn't get and focusing on what we did. This form of denial is a survival mechanism designed to lift us out of the pain of our young and sensitive hearts. Unless the acts of violence against us were outrageous or truly horrendous, we will, more than likely, minimize the amount of damage done to us by those we love, those who loved us, and those who had access to us as we grew up. We will justify others' behaviors because to acknowledge them in their entirety would be equivalent to giving ourselves the compassion that we rightly deserve—which may be the single most difficult task for us to take on. Although many of us have already acknowledged the pain of our past, if we are still beating ourselves up by self-sabotaging (in even one aspect of our lives), being a victim, or staying stuck in an old emotional pattern that is robbing us of joy and contentment, our challenge is to look deeper. More than likely, these patterns are the result of some hidden pain that we are still denying.

The sobering truth is that most of us do blame others for the continued suffering and misery we experience in our day-to-day lives, whether we want to or not, whether consciously or unconsciously. But when we are self-sabotaging—blowing up our dreams, acting out in inappropriate ways; or, if we find ourselves time and time again in the wreckage of someone else's self-sabotage, we are probably holding some deep-seated resentment that we are in denial about.

If we are to have any hope of breaking free from the trance of denial, we must first learn to distinguish its seductive internal voice. This voice—although we may argue to the contrary—is really not that distinctive for any one of us. The voice of denial for those who are victims, who find themselves being preyed upon by others, sounds something like this: *It's not so bad. It could be worse. I must have done something wrong. He/she can't really be doing this to me. Things will change. I can change this. Maybe this will just go away. I can handle it. I know what I'm doing. It must be my fault. That's just the way people are. What can you do?*

The voice of denial for the victimizer, the predator, someone who is denying the harm that he or she is doing to another, is also quite universal. It might sound like this: *They deserve it. They should never have messed with me. They were asking for it. No one will know. No one will find out. It doesn't matter anyway. I couldn't help myself. The rules don't apply to me. If it wasn't me it would be someone else. I have every right because I was abused when I was young. Every man for himself. This is just the way business is done.*

The voice of denial for the person who is self-sabotaging might sound something like this: *I'll deal with this later. I have everything under control. Just one more time. A little bit won't hurt me. I'll clean up my act tomorrow. This is good for me. At least I'm not as bad as some people. I don't have time. It can wait.*

The murky water of denial has us believe our own thoughts even when others are trying hard to wake us up to the truth.

Denial puts us in a trancelike state, which is why it seems so real and why it is so difficult to break free of. It is the hardest state of consciousness to identify because its very function, its very job, is to convince us that we are not in it! But once we become fully conscious of the function of denial—to defend us from being further traumatized—we realize that its job is *not* to provide us with clarity but is in fact just the opposite. It's a brilliantly designed defense. It blinds us from the truth even when that truth is hurting us or others.

Perpetuating Denial

In a state of denial, we get to dismiss how badly we were hurt, and we don't have to admit to all the ways we have been violated and have violated others. Denial and justifications for other people's bad behaviors come in many forms. The most spiritual justification of the twentieth century is "They did the best they could." Is this always true? Did all of our parents, siblings, family, teachers, neighbors, friends, religious organizations, and society really do the best they could? Maybe they just did to us what had been done to them. Maybe they didn't know any better. Maybe ignorance is not a true crime.

But I ask you: If you kill a child's right to be a child, to experience their innocence, to enjoy the moment, to express all of themselves (as long as they are not hurting someone else, of course), couldn't that be considered a crime? Why do we allow crimes of the spirit to go unpunished? Why do we deny the depth of the emotional, psychological, and spiritual abuse that goes on each and every day? May I tell you why? Because if we didn't deny it, many of us would end up behind bars just for the way we treat ourselves. It's a harsh reality that we must wake up to. We are living in a collective trance that says it's OK to beat up on others, ourselves, and the world at large. And the cost of this collective and unspoken trance is that the cycle of pain and victimization lives on. We continue being our own worst enemies and living under the illusion that we are powerless to do anything about it. If we don't wake up we will continue to blame our weaknesses and misdeeds on others. We will continue to deny our power and the importance of our behavior on the world around us. And, even more costly, we will be unable to really hold others accountable for their actions because we won't want to hold *ourselves* accountable for our part in the destruction of the human spirit. Thus the adage "I won't tell if you don't tell." We continue to turn our backs on ourselves and on others because we feel powerless to do anything about the endless cycles of abuse. Then, with our eyes closed, we become a part of the very dynamic that we were wounded by, and we become blind to the ways we participate in the abuse. Not only do we participate in the killing of the spirits of others; we become the chief offender in killing ourselves—emotionally, psychologically, physically, and spiritually. We unknowingly adopt the beliefs of our perpetrators and then carry out the offense over and over again, until we can no longer hear the voice of our true essence or even recognize our greatness.

We participate in the destruction of our own spirit by listening to the life-draining, negative internal messages that disempower and shame us over and over again. We participate by taking responsibility for crimes against ourselves that we had nothing to do with. We participate by robbing ourselves of our highest expression, hiding our God-given gifts, withholding our opinions, and taking to heart the shame-filled messages of our damaged and toxic minds. We participate by putting foods in our bodies that make us sick and taking drugs (prescription and otherwise) that we don't need. We participate by keeping ourselves separate and isolating ourselves from those we love or those who love us. We do it by denying our sexuality and then acting out in inappropriate or harmful sexual behaviors such as cheating on our spouses, having anonymous sex, indulging in pornography (including child porn), and other distortions of our sexuality. We do it by focusing all of our precious energy on others' lives rather than our own. We do it by filling our lives with idle gossip and tabloid trash. We do it by comparing ourselves to others and focusing on unobtainable images and goals. We do it by being too busy and taking on too much. We do it by not finishing what we started or not even starting that which we dream about. We do it by denying our dreams and staying in jobs that we despise. We do it by failing to acknowledge all that we do and all that we are. Each time we participate in the killing off of our most magnificent self, we further perpetuate the shame that drives our behaviors and ultimately our lives.

We participate in the killing off of our spirits by perpetuating the lies that have been delivered to us in so many ways—the lies being the beliefs we hold about ourselves. But it's now time to break free from denial and start telling the truth. Your beliefs, even the ones deeply ingrained in your psyche, are not *the* truth, they are *a* truth—and they can also be a lie. It's a lie when you refuse to see the entire picture, and when you're in denial you are seeing only part of the picture rather than its entirety. It's a lie when you shut out other realities and stay transfixed in a half truth or a limited perspective. This is denial!

The events of our past caused each of us to buy in to many lies about ourselves. Maybe you were overweight in the fourth grade and were the last person picked for the relay team. At that moment, feeling the shame of not being good enough, you unknowingly bought in to a lie about yourself. The denial switch flipped on and blinded you to the part of you that *is* good enough. Maybe your mom walked out on you when you were three years old and you decided that she left because you are unlovable. Then, no matter how much love people tried to give you, you couldn't let it in because you already bought the lie, a half truth born out of a limited perspective that left you firmly ensconced in denial about some part of yourself. It's time to recognize these lies for what they are and acknowledge the deeper truth: beliefs are just that—beliefs. Our beliefs have been adopted by us and ingrained into our psyches. It doesn't matter whether we adopted them from our parents, our teachers, or our religious leaders. We just need to understand that we have them and that they are only part of us and part of the truth about who we are. We do not have to spend the rest of our lives in denial, being directed by limiting beliefs that interfere with our joy, our state of well-being, our success, and our highest expression. The beliefs that we are not enough, that there is something wrong with us, that we are damaged and don't deserve to live a fully expressed life are just a few of the collective lies that we hold in our shame body. These lies that we tell ourselves shame us, confirming the untruth that we are really the bad ones who should go without love, money, health, or happiness.

We perpetuate these lies every time we remain in the victim state and don't have the strength to stand up and shout, "I'm not going to take it anymore. I am not going to listen to the negative messages of my past. I am not going to continue the abuse, nor am I going to take the abuse of others anymore." Yes, we are the ones who need help, because we can't change what happened to us ten, twenty, or thirty years ago, or even two months ago. We are the ones who have to be willing to go to any lengths to break free from the trance of denial. Until we do, the pain that we are unwilling to acknowledge and feel will bind us to our wounded ego's mask, and therefore to our limitations.

Our only option if we want to ensure that we stay present to what's really going on around us is to constantly check in with ourselves and others, ask for honest feedback, and search through our own internal closets to see if there is something we are hiding from or avoiding. We must be willing to make tough choices, ask for and listen to feedback, admit to our vulnerabilities, accept our own limitations, and get help when we need it. If we are not willing to be this rigorous, we have no hope of living an authentic, soul-filled, impassioned life.

Enabling Denial

When we're in denial, we have no ability to see how "off" our behaviors really are—like in the Michael Jackson saga. Here was a grown man inviting young children to sleep in his bed, and their parents were allowing this. He didn't think there was anything wrong with his actions, but clearly someone should have.

When one or more people come together in denial, bad things almost always happen. People who are acting out in destructive and damaging ways can be allowed to continue for months and even years, enabled by our denial about what they are doing. If we are denying, rationalizing, or dismissing the actions of those who hurt innocent people, we are committing a crime as well. How often do we sense that bad things are happening to our neighbors and loved ones, but we turn our heads or righteously claim that it's none of our business? Denial will argue that other people's problems have nothing to do with us—that we are good people minding our own business. Our denial convinces us we are doing the best we can to manage our own lives and it would be a great inconvenience to stop and help them out.

Again, it's so easy to point our fingers at others rather than to stand up and admit that sometimes other people's problems are ours as well. Here are a few sobering examples: A child of a good family is acting out, doing drugs and getting into trouble. When the parents first find out, they step in to help, horrified, scared, and wanting to keep their child safe. They might bring their child to therapy but see no need to go themselves. They don't take the time to dig around into their own issues because they are in denial that their child's problems have anything to do with them. The child continues to get in trouble, ripping people off, causing property damage to friends' homes, and it goes on and on. Nothing the mother or father says seems to help the child. So at some point the parents decide they're just going to love him no matter what he does. Now they are firmly rooted in a reality they believe to be consistent with that of "good parents" and are in complete denial about the pain their son causes others. With each incident they find out about, they continue to deny the damage their son is inflicting on others, and slowly they begin to rationalize why he is so troubled. Their rationalization allows another veil of denial to take form so they don't have to feel the shame of having a child who is out of control—or worse, so they won't feel the shame and devastation of being a failure as a parent.

Confronting the reality of the situation is just too painful, so instead they try to help their poor, wounded son. They get him good jobs, lying (by not exposing their son's issues) to people who might be able to help their precious offspring get out of this rut. The disease of denial has spread; now they're lying not just to themselves but to others as well. But of course to them their fabrications are not really a lie, because they are just withholding the truth. When friends and family members who know a little bit about (we'll call him Don) Don's troubled past ask, "How is Don?" they lie, saying that things are better and Don is doing great. Soon Don is a grown man in his thirties, in business with one of his parents' friends and cheating them out of money. Once again, he winds up in financial trouble, and once again his parents bail him out. They no longer think about all the other people whom their son is hurting; in fact they don't even want to know (another form of denial). They now only want to save face and protect their own broken hearts from being further broken, never stopping to think about whom Don will hurt in the future as a result of their enabling him. So now I ask you, who is the bad person here? Who is the con artist and the co-conspirator? Isn't enabling someone to act out and victimize another also a form of victimization? This is where we can see how we are all co-conspirators and how our need to avoid feeling our own shame and pain has us become so self-absorbed and selfish that we can't even see—let alone take responsibility for—the effect that our denial has on others. Maybe you can't relate to the story of the enabling parents, but if you have grown children you might want to look at how you participate in their denial about some part of their life that is not working or how they participate in yours.

John is a retired real estate agent who now sues innocent people for a living. For over ten years his son Ronnie has known the truth that others in his family have tried to deny: his dad doesn't really have a job or a business. John is always talking about one business idea after another that never comes to fruition. Whenever Ronnie gets upset or frustrated with his father, he brings this fact up, questioning John about what he really does to maintain his opulent lifestyle. But when John shows signs of defensiveness, letting his anger rear its ugly head (nobody who is in denial likes to be questioned), Ronnie backs down because the benefits he reaps from his father's lies prevent him from wanting to know the truth about his father's shady business affairs. Ronnie constantly suppresses his intuitive knowing that there is something wrong and hides his suspicions from both his father and himself. And yet he watches his father luring one group of people after another into participating in the next big business venture, each time seeing the deals fall apart and hearing about the ugly lawsuits that follow. Because of his shame, Ronnie has to build his father up, magnifying his father's strengths and denying his father's weaknesses, in order to keep his denial intact. When Ronnie does pop out of denial from time to time, he feels such hopelessness and resentment that he ends up sabotaging his own goals in order not to show his father up. Now he and his father collude to keep each other in denial, afraid that if they tell the truth they will lose each other's love. Again I ask you, is Ronnie participating in the crimes of his father—knowingly or unknowingly? Does he have any responsibility to the outsiders he sees his father bring into his life—knowing that more than likely they will be hurt or even destroyed by his father? Now aware of the giant integrity issue of being a co-conspirator with his father, Ronnie can't stop his own self-sabotage. To date Ronnie continues to fail because he is still unwilling to suffer what he believes will be the consequences of telling the truth.

Jill and Steve have been married for twelve years. Steve is a college professor, and Jill is a hotshot photographer who drinks too much. She is strong-willed, outspoken, and known as a force to be reckoned with. For the last eight years, Jill's drinking has progressively worsened. A few times a year she embarrasses herself, slurring her words at charity functions and making a slight public spectacle of herself. However, because Steve and Jill donate a lot of money to their community, everyone around them keeps their mouths shut about Jill's behavior. What only Steve and a few others know is that every time Jill embarrasses herself publicly she becomes inwardly ashamed of herself and outwardly more and more aggressive. Her strategy to avoid dealing with her own bad behavior is to attack others. Her attacks are always on those she feels are not as strong as she is, those she can use to take the attention off herself and project her inadequacies on.

Even though many people know the truth about her, her power and position intimidate them into keeping their mouths shut. Someone could work for five months on a beautiful event, and if Jill just happened to have a bad night, publicly shaming herself, one of the people on the committee of that event would inevitably be destroyed by Jill's gossip, innuendos, or out-and-out accusations. Everyone around her knows the truth—Steve certainly knows—and yet no one is willing to do a thing. Their justification? "Look at all the good things Jill is doing for the community." "If I confront her I might be the next one to go down, or the charity whose board I sit on will be minus a big donation next year." "I don't want to be the only one who doesn't get invited to Jill and Steve's famous Fourth of July party." Because those around her are not willing to deal with the consequences of telling the truth, they go into denial, minimize the effects of Jill's behavior, and relieve themselves of any responsibility for her actions. This only enables her to continue with the destructive pattern that hurts not only herself, but other innocent people as well. Now let's look again. Are those who deny the impact of Jill's pattern at all responsible for or co-conspirators in the next victim's pain? The wounded, shameful self (always protecting itself with denial) would say no. "After all," it maintains, "I didn't do anything, and it's none of my business anyway."

In the desperate attempt to feel better about itself, our wounded ego seeks to be right. It is always looking for evidence of why its thoughts, desires, and actions are justified. It judges others continuously but can't seem to see itself from any perspective other than its own. It looks for ways to justify its behavior or, even worse, to deny it altogether. This is why so many people don't ask for the help they need, and why they can so easily ridicule and demonize other people, their views, their beliefs, and their actions—all the while staying mired in their own denial.

The Shame of Denial

The cover of the December 22, 2002, issue of *Time* magazine read, "The Whistleblowers," and underneath this title was a picture of the three women who brought down Enron. Now excuse me, but is this term—*whistle-blower*—a badge of honor? Is this the best America could do for the three women who were courageous enough to take down the biggest business fraud in the history of the United States? Shouldn't we have titled it "The Heroes, the Goddesses, the Brave" or "The Superwomen"? Now, I'm sure not everyone took this title as badly as I did, but I felt deeply saddened that this was the best we could do for these women. I felt I had to take some responsibility for the culture I live in because I had never stood up and challenged people around the world to become superheroes—that is, whistle-blowers. I had already written five books, so I could have done something to change the way we look at whistle-blowers. I never even wrote a note to *Time* letting the editors know how I felt about the title they chose to portray these women and what they did. In fact, I had exactly the opposite reaction. I felt deeply ashamed for the "tattletale" in me, which is why I am exposing it now. When I saw the cover of the magazine, my first thought was, *I don't want to be that.* My shame directed my choice to do nothing. My fear of the whistle-blower in me made my stomach cringe and the little girl inside who wants to do the right thing shrink. It brought up all the times I spoke up and then got shamed, put down, or shunned for it.

The cosmic joke, of course, is that I *am* a whistle-blower. Isn't that what I am doing right now? Am I not calling to task all of the denied and rejected parts of us that are out there, consciously or unconsciously, directly or indirectly, adding to the pain in this world? Isn't that what I do every time I coax a shadow out of hiding? I can't help myself. I am always trying to bring the bad guys out into the open, exposing them for who they really are, even when it hurts me. There have been hundreds of times in the past ten years when I wished I could have just kept my big mouth shut—but I can't. The more I awaken from the automatic trance of my shame body, the more compelled I am to act on behalf of the collective whole rather than for my own individual self. This means relinquishing my small, selfish perspective and becoming a shameless global citizen (a person more committed to the good of the collective whole than to their own individual comfort). I believe that this is the person I was born to be—that we were all born to be: caring, loving, brave, authentic, and awake to the needs of the world.

When we were kids and we witnessed mean play on the school playground, we probably automatically said, "Don't do that!" or "That's not OK!" If there was an abusive person in our households when we were growing up, we tried to defend our mother, our sisters, or our brothers. We wanted to make it all OK. It was and still is our innate desire to prevent those around us from imploding or exploding and to protect strangers from being hurt; we're good, and we want to help. But then we were told over and over again to mind our own business. We tried to fix a bad situation, and we were told to keep our mouths shut or butt out. We wanted to tell the teacher when Barry threw a rock at Bobby on the playground, but then they called us a tattletale and that felt awful, shameful, and painful. The embarrassment made us question our good nature. We questioned whether it was worth it to intervene in someone's bad behavior, or to tell someone who had the power, "Stop it." We questioned whether we were doing the right thing when we tried to put a stop to the injustices we saw all around us and were taunted and teased instead. Accused and made wrong for standing up for others, we shrank and slipped back into denial. We hid part of our light, our ever-loving goodness, so that we could fit in and not have to suffer the consequences of another's bad behavior. After all, we were just trying to help.

We can all sit back self-righteously and watch others do bad things. We can turn our heads and pretend we are innocent because we have not participated directly in acts of violence against another person. But are we really innocent? Or are we just in denial? We want to hold our government and higher authorities accountable, but why don't we want to hold those around us and ourselves to that same level of accountability?

What if in breaking free of your own denial you could stop someone from victimizing another? What if you could prevent someone else from becoming a victim? What if the person you save has the key to heal our planet so our kids and our grandkids will have a safe place to live? Then would you do something? Then would you use your voice? What would be important enough to you for you to step in and make a difference? Who would you have to be in order to have your eyes wide open, out of denial, and take a stand for those who are going to be the next victims? And what are the costs and the consequences of keeping your mouth shut? Does it just add to your own shame body, unknowingly draining your life force, robbing you of the dignity and self-respect you so deeply desire? Or is there an even greater cost?

Let us be inspired by the words of our brother Dr. Martin Luther King Jr., who refused to sit back and keep his mouth shut. One man was able to help an entire nation break out of denial and step into the light of the truth. His voice was what some considered loud, pushy, and aggressive. But his outrage and his fearlessness caused a massive awakening in our world. Dr. King showed us what one man, one life, could do when denial is no longer an option. He asked us to break free from the bonds of a limited perspective that millions had bought in to and to stand up as beacons of light for the good of all, which caused a revolution of change. It is the very best in us that stands up and shouts out in protest to the collective shadow that keeps us small and our universal eyes closed. Today, we must remember the great leaders of global change who have lived before us and allow their words and their courage to live on in our actions. We must decide, en masse, that we will no longer keep our eyes shut and our mouths closed. If popping out of denial will return you to your innate power and help the life of an innocent victim, are you willing to do it now? Or are you too ensconced in your own pain to worry about anyone else?

More and more people will continue to do bad things to themselves and others as long as we as a culture refuse to be accountable and continue to enable others. It's unbelievable how many of us conspire to keep people in business who are actively and knowingly hurting others. It's happening in our churches, our synagogues, and other religious organizations. It's happening in charities and in big and small businesses around the world. It's happening in our governments, our hospitals, our judicial system, and our prisons. It is happening in our schools and very often right here within our own families. It's happening. And every time we turn our backs, we are colluding with the perpetrators, the "bad guys." Even those who are conscious can't help themselves when the perpetrator is persuasive and likable (and many of them are) or when the person doing bad things is doing some good things as well. We are so consumed with our own comfort levels that we don't put the well-being of the whole, the collective (meaning all other human beings, the ones we know and the ones we don't know), into the equation by which we measure our deeds.

Recently I was having this discussion with a girlfriend of mine. In one moment she was agreeing that we all have to face our own discomfort and start standing up for each other, and then less then five minutes later she slipped back into denial. She told me about a friend of hers who was about to go to jail for four years for draining his business of all its assets and ripping off his investors for more than $25 million. One minute she was feeling bad for all the families that would now have to suffer the consequences of her friend's actions, and the very next she told me she was planning a dinner party to send this man off to prison. She couldn't help herself. I don't even know this man, but when I challenged the integrity of her throwing a party for a convicted felon and asked her to view this choice through the eyes of all this man's victims, she conceded that giving him a party was a selfish thing to do. Her smile said it all: "He's a funny guy with lots of charm [by the way, most con men have charm in spades], and he makes me feel good." So here it was, right in front of my face: a self-serving, evil man to the people he preyed upon, but to his "close" friends a charming, fun guy to hang out with. And then out of my friend's mouth came the enabler's mantra: "But maybe he didn't mean it!"

If we won't make the change, who will? If we are going to continue pretending that the bad ones live "out there," without taking responsibility for the ways we participate in bringing harm to others, our personal quest to be good is futile. If we keep our eyes sealed shut, we are as much a part of the problem as the victimizer next door. Why not stop trying so hard to convince ourselves that we are good and just become one of the walking numb who shut out and shut themselves off from their personal responsibility? Why don't we all stop pretending (if indeed we are) that we are working for the good of all, since nothing will ever change if it doesn't start right here at home? It's one of those crazy things where we work and work and work "out there" to do something good and then use our frenzied activity as an excuse not to deal with that which we can directly affect right now. All the good deeds in the world won't wipe out the damage that goes unattended in our own backyard.

10

HEALING
THE SPLIT

When the pressure of our repressed darkness becomes too great, when the depth of our self-hatred and shame gets overwhelming, we put ourselves at risk of making unconscious choices that will expose our wounds—causing us to finally get the help we so desperately need. It's usually only after we are confronted in no uncertain terms with the wreckage of our wounded ego that the veil of our denial is lifted and the healing process can begin. When we hit the wall and the pain of our shame is too much to bear, a door opens that allows us to reunite with our higher self and become the integrated being that is part of the spiritual solution. Whether we are the victim or the victimizer, predator or prey, the healing process is the same. To heal the internal war between these opposing forces, we have to step out of denial, own up to our essential nature, expose our weaknesses, uncover our blind spots, and tell the truth about our human tendencies. Only after we've made an honest assessment will we be able to see what we need to do to balance our nature—to strengthen our weaknesses and curb our negative impulses.

If you're a victim but can't admit that you're a victim, if you are a prey type but pretend that you aren't, you will never be responsible enough to arm yourself with the resources you need to ensure your own protection. To the extent that you remain in denial about your true nature, you will continue to be victimized, abused, betrayed, fooled, or taken advantage of. And although as prey you appear to others as an obvious victim, I'm going to suggest that you are also a victimizer. As long as you fail to take responsibility for your gullible nature and protect your vulnerable heart, you will unconsciously continue to victimize yourself for crimes you didn't even commit. And in the process you hurt not only yourself but those around you who watch powerlessly as you are taken advantage of or put yourself at the mercy of one unfortunate incident after another. Denial is what allows the cycle of abuse to continue. If you are a prey type, the only way to put an end to this cycle of victimization is to look squarely at the truth, admit who you are, and take measurable steps to protect your vulnerable nature.

If you are a victimizer, your task is to tell the truth about your dark impulses, your predatory tendencies, and the ways you consciously or unconsciously con, lie, manipulate, deceive, hurt, use, or take advantage of others. You must wake yourself up to the cost of your actions. As long as you are unwilling or unable to admit that you are a predator, you will remain blind to the extent of the damage you inflict on others and also on yourself. The hidden truth is that every predator is also prey. Most

likely you yourself were the victim of an abuser, a violent or un-
stable upbringing, or your society as a whole. As a victimizer you
must realize that as long as you continue to hurt others you are
also sealing in your fate as your own worst enemy. You will be
the one left in the wake of the destruction that you create for
others, and you will be the one left with the haunting shame
that will constantly remind you of your bad deeds. By coming
to terms with your predatory nature, you can provide this aspect of yourself with healthy, safe, and appropriate outlets for
expression. You can put structures in place that ensure that you
don't violate the boundaries of others or act out in inappropriate
ways. You can get the help you might need to ensure that your
actions don't continue to hurt others.

I want to reiterate this point: the healing process for the victim and the victimizer is the same. The wounded ego can't heal
without the insight, understanding, and wisdom of the higher
self. By bringing forth the love and compassion of the higher self
to both the dark and the light, the victim and the victimizer, the
predator and prey that live within us, we become integrated and
emotionally healthy human beings. It is then that the split between the two sides of ourselves is mended and we return to our
true essence. When the sabotaging and destructive nature of
the wounded self merges with the healing power of the higher
self, this integration occurs.

The higher self has the capability, the power, and the strength
to see from a broader perspective, to see through spiritual eyes,
to know that every negative quality, impulse, and tendency has
an equal and opposite counterpart that can be cultivated to bring
us back into a state of balance. Healing the split requires us to
be firmly rooted in the reality that duality is central to our very

nature. We couldn't know light unless we knew darkness; we wouldn't know courage unless we experienced fear. We would never recognize a kind heart had we not encountered a mean one. We could never know hope if we hadn't experienced the devastation of hopelessness. In this world of duality, the way we understand and gain wisdom is through comparison and contrast. So ultimately this journey is one of coming into balance with these seemingly opposing expressions of our humanity and learning to recognize the early warning signs that alert us when our inner world is out of balance.

Signposts of Disaster

The only way for us to ensure that we stay on the right path rather than get lured down the road of our dark side is to remain constantly aware of all of the tendencies within us that hold the power to lead us astray. I've identified seven ways of being that, when ignored, can engage us in patterns of self-destruction. It is the devastation created by our guardedness, greed, arrogance, intolerance, self-absorption, stubbornness, and deceit that separates us from our higher selves. And whereas these tendencies can lead to our ultimate demise, finding their counterbalance will heal our internal split and return us to wholeness, where once again we can bask in the totality of all of who we are.

Within each of us is both prey and predator, and we must open our hearts to both of these parts of ourselves. If we don't accept the duality of our human nature, it's impossible for us to heal. But as we recognize our tendencies and our weaknesses, and bring the awareness and compassion of our higher self to these parts, we bridge the separation that leads us down a road of self-destruction, and we allow the healthy integration of all aspects of us to emerge.

The process is one of balancing the seesaw—neutralizing the tendencies within us that have gone out of balance and allowing the peaceful coexistence of all parts of us. Then our loving, good impulses are balanced with our dark, self-serving impulses. This is what it is to be an integrated human being

There is nothing more inspiring than a wounded ego that has been rejoined with its healthy counterpart. When our lower self and our divine essence are reunited, we can heal, mend, transcend, and thrive—even in the worst of circumstances. But for this healing to begin, the ego must make room for our higher self to enter back into the picture.

I was recently presenting at a conference along with Dr. Dean Ornish, Clinical Professor of Medicine at the University of San Francisco, and the author of five books, including *Love and Survival.* I sat in on Dean's lecture and during his talk he showed a slide, which illustrated an important concept that he had learned from one of his mentors. The slide had the following two words written on it:

illness
wellness

He asked the audience to reflect on the difference between these two words and then, after a brief pause, he moved to the next slide. The two words were written again, only the "I" in illness and the "we" in wellness were circled, like this:

(i)llness
(we)llness

Here it was right in front of me—the problem and the solution. The problem, which we have examined at length throughout this book, arises when we are identified solely with the "I," with the limited perspective of our individual selves. When we are viewing life through the lens of our own narcissistic tendencies, we only care about what will serve ourselves. We literally do not perceive any choices other than the ones that we believe will fulfill our individual emotional or physical needs—no matter how destructive or unhealthy they might be.

When we begin to understand that our "I" consciousness, our ego, is only a portion of who we are, we open ourselves up to merging with the "we," which is what I call the collective heart. "We" is the part of us that is connected to all that is, and to every other human being. It's the part of us that is willing to make a higher choice, even when it doesn't feel good to our individual "I." This collective part of us knows that to be truly happy and whole, we must respond to a higher calling and surrender our personal agendas for the benefit of the collective good.

To the extent that we are preoccupied with making it, with looking good, with fitting in, succeeding, belonging, winning, or trying to get what we think should be ours, we lock ourselves into the small cage of our individual self. Our overidentification with "I" is the source of all our trauma, pain, and self-sabotage. It is the source of our illness, which drives us to sabotage our dreams and become our own worst enemy.

When we are willing to open up and explore "we" consciousness; when we begin to look for ways to serve, connect, and support others; when we see how our actions can benefit all concerned and commit ourselves to living in partnership with the greater whole, we return to our natural truest authentic state. We return to wellness and regain the ability to live meaningful, passion-filled lives, follow the guidance of our higher selves, take right action, and make better choices than we would when we are only looking through the small lens of our individual self.

When the ego resumes its rightful place—when it occupies half of our identity rather than overtaking the whole—the higher self can give the ego the vulnerability, generosity, humility, compassion, willingness, and integrity it needs to make peace with its flaws, weaknesses, and human tendencies. It is in this moment that the wounded part of the ego can heal and the unification process between the light and the dark can begin. Then the good self and the bad, the Dr. Jekyll and Mr. Hyde, the true self and the false, the "I" and "we" can work together in the graceful dance called a human life. When all parts of ourselves are given permission to coexist, we have the wisdom to make the highest evolutionary choices for ourselves and those around us day after day. When the ego and the higher self act as allied forces, we heal the internal split that causes us to act as our own worst enemies and come to rest once again on the solid ground of the unified self. Here we have access to abundant emotional, physical, intellectual, and spiritual well-being.

To live a soul-driven rather than an ego-driven life, we must be alert to seven states of being that have the ability to steer us off course and back into the ego's grip. Guardedness, greed, arrogance, intolerance, self-absorption, stubbornness, and deceit are seven states of being that indicate that our wounded ego is now in control and is acting out autonomously. When any one of these particular states of being dominates our awareness, it acts as a warning that our inner world is dangerously out of balance and that if we do not take immediate action, disaster is near. These seven signposts are the powerful, sometimes hidden catalysts that drive good people to do bad things. You'll notice that each of them arises when we are identified only with our individual self, our "I."

Each of these signposts is a natural state of being that we will all more than likely experience at some point in our lives. Remember, we are all human, and we all possess every human quality, every human emotion, and every state of being. And depending on the nature of our ego's wounds, certain tendencies will arise within us, at different times and in different situations, that will drive us to act in particular ways. When these seven states of being are balanced with their polar opposites— their spiritual antidotes—they become neutralized. This means we have a choice to experience and use them at will. But when these tendencies are left without the weight of their counterpart to keep them in check, we are powerless to control them. In other words, they control us rather than us controlling them.

Because these tendencies exist within each of us, none of us is immune to their potentially dangerous effects. However, each of these signposts can be brought into balance by consciously cultivating its polar opposite and invoking its spiritual antidote. Generosity is the antidote that balances our tendency to be greedy. Humility is the antidote that softens our arrogance. Vulnerability is the antidote to being overly guarded. Being of service balances our tendency to be self-absorbed. Honesty is the antidote to our tendency toward deceit. Willingness is the antidote that softens our stubborn nature. Compassion is the antidote that balances our intolerance. The antidotes transcend our limited "I" perspective, bringing us back into alignment with our higher selves and into the collective heart.

The Signposts of Disaster are like a "Road Closed" sign warning us that we are headed for trouble. They caution us to beware and to keep the darker impulses of our humanity in check. If we fail to heed these warnings, self-sabotage is the unfortunate result.

The Antidotes are the spiritual thread that mends the split between our dark side and our highest self. When we allow them to work in our lives, we neutralize and counteract our destructive tendencies and moment by moment, choice by choice, guide ourselves toward a more honest and authentically fulfilling life.

Signpost No. 1: Guardedness

Gripped by the fear that somebody is going to expose us, hurt us, take advantage of us, shame us, humiliate us, embarrass us, use us, or exploit our weaknesses, we become guarded. While self-protection is important in times of actual danger, being overly guarded presents hazards of its own. Feeling guarded, we construct thick walls around ourselves—walls that prevent us from being intimate, from asking for help or trusting that we can share our darker thoughts, feelings, and impulses with others. We hear, "Beware—they're out to get you!" as we look around every corner, suspecting everyone and everything. Guardedness tells us that we will be exposed or taken advantage of if we let ourselves be seen. And in our attempt to protect our vulnerability and hide our shame, we disconnect from a vital feedback loop—the perspectives of others.

In our guarded state, it becomes all too easy to surrender to our delusional thoughts, sink into our denial, and act on our distorted impulses. Guardedness is so dangerous because it separates us from those who could actually help us. When we are operating from a guarded, self-protective place, we become oblivious to the bigger world, defensive, isolated, distrustful, argumentative, and secretive—to name just a few qualities. As we begin to question whom we can talk to and what parts of ourselves or our lives are safe to disclose, we are driven deeper and deeper into secrecy about who we are, what we do, and how we really feel. We feel too afraid to open up and too ashamed to allow ourselves to be seen and known by others. Our guarded stance is created and then fueled by thoughts like, *If they find out about me I'm in trouble. What did they mean by that? They're going to hurt me.* The biggest danger of our guarded state is that it has us create an increasingly small world around ourselves to keep our persona intact and our secrets hidden. When the wounds of our ego have made our human self and its dark impulses wrong, we feel unsafe, scared, and ashamed and begin to separate from those around us. First we separate from the world at large, then from our community, and finally from our inner circle of family and friends. The more guarded we become, the more intensely we fear being found out.

When we guard ourselves to the point where we are no longer able to be vulnerable, to admit to our unhealthy impulses, and to ask for the help we might need, we contaminate our relationships, filling them with mistrust and, eventually, paranoia and deceit. Guardedness, without the balance of vulnerability, leads to isolation. Isolation is a red flag warning us that we have disconnected from ourselves, others, and the laws of the world. It is a precursor to becoming our own worst enemies. Our secrets will always keep us sick and stuck in the grip of our wounded egos.

THE SPIRITUAL ANTIDOTE: VULNERABILITY

One of the most important functions of a healthy ego is to know its strengths and weaknesses, to sense when the time is right to go it alone and when we should ask for help. But in our guarded stance, we are so busy trying to keep people from finding out about some aspect of our lives, we become unable to see ourselves clearly, monitor our behaviors objectively, or ask for the support we need. When this happens, we put ourselves in great danger.

The truth is, we are designed to function as part of a greater whole. We need the input of others in order to gain a clear view of ourselves. The feedback we receive as a result of connecting with those around us provides an important reference point that helps us know where we stand with ourselves and the world. Guardedness cuts us off from this valuable feedback loop, and the only way we can open up to it again is to take down some of our walls and become vulnerable enough to let people in.

Inside the self-protective stance of the ego, we hate to admit that we need anything or anyone, so we end up building thicker and thicker walls to convince ourselves of our strength. But when we embrace our vulnerable nature, we are able to reach out to others, to depend on others. Vulnerability gives us the freedom to admit, "I need you." It takes courage to get out of denial about who we are, what we need, and what our weaknesses are. Yet being vulnerable enough to admit these things is the only way to keep our dark side in check and ensure that we are acting from our highest selves.

You might be one of the people who confuse vulnerability with weakness, but true vulnerability is a sign of strength. It takes a degree of vulnerability to approach life with an open heart and to allow yourself to intimately connect with those around you. Your vulnerable self is the most innocent part of you, the child-like part of you that wants only to be good and to belong.

To be vulnerable is to be human, and to deny this part of yourself or shield it by being shut down keeps you from being open to receiving the very things that you long for the most. The spiritual antidote of vulnerability awakens in us the aware-ness that our only safety lies in absolute defenselessness of our human weaknesses. In our state of vulnerability we allow God to do for us what we can't do for ourselves.

Signpost No. 2: Greed

Fear of scarcity is at the root of our greed. Fueled by our fear that there isn't enough love, money, opportunities, or material possessions to go around, greed causes us to crave more and more. Fear of being poor, fear that our needs won't be met, or fear of failing triggers our greed and drives us to make sure we get ours, no matter what the cost. Our healthy greed might mo-tivate us to be successful, while an inbalance of greed will drive us to amass wealth simply to prove that we are worthwhile. When our greedy nature is out of balance and running our lives, we are perpetually hungry—for love, money, status, approval, possessions, and power.

Our greed is what seduces us into believing the illusion that satisfaction exists "out there" in the external world. We become a bottomless pit, believing we will be OK as soon as we get "enough." Too much greed drives us to meet our own needs—

emotional, sexual, financial, or otherwise—regardless of the effect our behaviors have on those around us. Greed tells us we will be OK as soon as we attain the next conquest. We insatiably consume more in an attempt to satisfy our hunger for things outside ourselves, even if this means breaking the law. Blinded to anything but our own needs, we allow our greed to lead us down a path of consumption that will bring about our own demise.

It takes a fair amount of self-examination to uncover where in our lives we have an imbalance of greed. We might be greedy for love, admiration, or attention. We might lust after being the smartest or the one with the most creative ideas. Our greed might show up around food, our need for fun, or even self-pity as we greedily seek the sympathy of others. Greed might manifest itself as possessiveness toward our friends, children, partners, or spouses.

Our greedy self, when out of balance, denies us the experience of living in a win-win universe as it seeks out ways to prevail—even if this means lying, cheating, or stealing. It can cost us our self-respect, our relationships, and inner peace. The cosmic joke is that as long as our greedy nature is left unchecked, we can never really experience satisfaction and fill our insatiable hunger, because we will always be seeking more, even just a few hours after we have fed it a big meal. When we fail to balance our ego's greedy nature by being generous, we are destined to act out in inappropriate ways, trying to take everything for ourselves while disregarding the needs of others.

THE SPIRITUAL ANTIDOTE: GENEROSITY

When our greedy nature is balanced by generosity, we are grounded in our deepest truth. Whereas greed tells us there is not enough, generosity asserts that there is enough for us all—an abundance of love, money, and success. When we are out of balance and cut off from our loving hearts and generous nature, we grasp for everything we can get our hands on—power, attention, love—even if it rightfully belongs to someone else. Our greedy tendencies are always asking, "What do you have for me?" while our generous nature asks, "What can I do for you?" When we balance our greedy selves with the good-heartedness of generosity, we are blessed with the ability to ask for what we deserve and to trust that there is enough for us all. Being generous—with our attention, with our kindness, with our talents, with our money—is a demonstration of our faith that there is enough for everyone, and in this state of faith, our cup runneth over.

Although being generous can involve the giving of financial wealth, food, clothing, gifts, and other goods, I'm going to assert that this is only part of the picture of generosity. Being generous doesn't mean we have to give large amounts of money. It doesn't mean we have to shower those around us with gifts and trinkets. Generosity encompasses a whole range of intangibles as well. Being generous means listening more attentively to others rather than greedily searching for opportunities to insert our beliefs and opinions into the conversation. When we are generous enough to take an interest in the thoughts, feelings, and activities of another, we leave our own self-interests behind and are actually able to hear the needs of those we love.

True generosity begins in the privacy of our own inner world; like everything else, it must begin at home. When we are generous with ourselves, we feel that we're worthy and valued. And when we feel worthy and valued, we automatically attract more of the good of the universe into our lives. When we're connected with the inherent generosity of the universe, our hearts are naturally more open and we feel safe to give and to receive. In this way, cultivating self-generosity supports us in understanding how to be more authentically generous with family members, friends, acquaintances, and strangers alike.

Generosity is the spiritual antidote that has the power to offset and balance our greedy nature. The good news about generosity is that it doesn't create any loss or lack for the giver. True generosity—anything that is given from the heart without attachment—is inevitably returned to the giver in kind. Generosity is an energetic transaction with the universe that will be repaid to us—most times, with interest. Openhearted giving works hand in hand with faith and gratitude as we learn that if we give, we will also receive. It arises naturally when we are connected with our higher selves.

Signpost No. 3: Arrogance

Our arrogant nature may disguise itself as grandiosity or enormous self-confidence, but in actuality it is rooted in inadequacy, insecurity, and fear. Arrogance is an expression of our obsession to be bigger, smarter, greater, and more important than other people in order to compensate for what we believe we lack. Because we feel so small and insignificant, we need to puff ourselves up in order to prove that we are, in fact, special. Trying to overcompensate for the fear that we are not good enough, we adopt a holier-than-thou attitude and may actually begin to believe we are better than those around us. Although arrogance may drive us to be more informed, more connected, and more successful, its motivation is to hide our weaknesses and exaggerate our strengths. Arrogance provides the perfect front, enabling us to be manipulative, irresponsible, controlling, and a rule breaker—just to name a few. It has us look down with condescension on those we have deemed less than we are. Arrogance leads us to believe we are above reproach and the rules do not apply to us. All dressed up in justifications and righteousness, our ego's arrogant tendencies seduce us into thinking we can do whatever we want and we won't be questioned or caught. Arrogance appears in our lives wearing many disguises. It shows itself in all the judgments we hold against others, it rears its head in our self-righteous bantering, and it keeps us loyal to what we believe to be the truth even when there is evidence to the contrary right before our eyes.

To uncover where and how our arrogance shows up, all we need to do is examine our judgments and projections. It is arrogant to judge others and think of ourselves as more evolved than they are. Anytime we find ourselves being affected by other people's behavior and thinking thoughts like, *They are stupid morons!* or *Why can't they just get it?!* this should be a red flag that we are projecting onto them some unwanted aspect of ourselves and that our arrogance is acting as a defense mechanism to keep us from seeing something about ourselves that we don't want to see. Whenever we are pointing our finger in self-righteousness, whenever we are sure that someone else is falling short of their potential, we must turn our gaze back upon ourselves. This requires the utmost of humility.

Arrogance without the spiritual antidote of humility leads to an impenetrable mind-set that cuts us off from honest self-evaluation and the ability to recognize our dark impulses, destructive tendencies, and what are—and are not—permissible behaviors. When acting on its own, our arrogant self shuts out any feedback from our higher self and from the outside world. When arrogance is dominating our awareness, we find ourselves moving with great confidence and at full speed—only in the wrong direction. Too sure of ourselves to consider another's point of view and too proud to ask for help when we need it, we allow arrogance to become the culprit that leads to many a downfall. All puffed up in full regalia, we feel for a moment that we are bigger than life. But as you know, the bigger we are, the harder we fall.

Believing that it knows best, our arrogant self can be spotted by its boasting, bullying, and defying the law. "I did it because I could" is the voice of our arrogance. A dose of humility is precisely what is needed to temper our arrogant nature and remind us that we are just one of 6 billion people on the planet and that the rules do apply to us as well. Humility balances arrogance and puts it in its place.

THE SPIRITUAL ANTIDOTE: HUMILITY

When we tap into our humble nature, we have a peaceful awareness of our place within the greater whole. Through humble eyes we are able to see the good intentions of others and celebrate—rather than compare and condemn—our differences. Humility makes us teachable and open to feedback, and it strengthens our ability to truly listen to ourselves and to others. It allows us to be open to not knowing and detached from the outcomes we once clung to for our sense of security. Humility gives us both the willingness to change and the vision to make the changes we need to make. Stripped of the false cloak of arrogance, we are humble enough to see ourselves as we are, and only then can we begin to envision the person we are capable of becoming.

With humility, our once rigid identity becomes more flexible, so we are no longer compelled to force ourselves and our views on others. Humility allows us to conserve the valuable energetic resources that we squander when we spend our time proving that we are superior to others. It frees us from the prison of competitively trying to one-up others and instead gives us permission to celebrate their accomplishments and differences.

Stripped of our arrogance, our justifications, and our righteousness, we can stand in the clear light of day without the shield of our false pride.

The humble part of us understands that we are no better or worse than anyone else. It understands that under different circumstances we could each be capable of exactly the things that we most want to judge others for doing. By cultivating humility, we learn to keep our attention on ourselves rather than spending our time focusing on the behaviors of others. True humility gives us the wisdom to avoid the trap of projecting our darkness onto others and allows us to be aware and accepting of our own imperfections and insecurities.

Humility allows us to embrace our perfections and our flaws with equal reverence. Until we are humble enough to admit that we have the same impulses as everyone else, and until we are at peace with all of our humanity—the dark as well as the light—we will continue to get blindsided by the arrogance of our wounded ego and create circumstances that devastate our lives. We will continue to manifest the very things we work so hard to avoid.

With the spiritual antidote of humility, we are able to let go of all that we do to prove ourselves to others. We are able to ask for help when needed. Our humble self doesn't waste a lot of energy resisting when things don't go our way, because it assumes that there is a grander order at work. With humility we give up the idea that we know what's best for ourselves. Humility frees us from the trap of getting caught up in our righteousness and judgments of others and allows us to merge with the collective whole. Humility invites us to keep our attention on ourselves and "change the things we can," instead of arrogantly trying to manage others' lives. In times of pain or confusion, humility allows us to drop to our hands and knees and ask for the support that we desperately need.

When our arrogant self is tempered by humility, we no longer have to participate in unnecessary boasting to prove our worth over and over to those around us. Instead we are free to live a simpler life, to focus on taking responsibility and maintaining integrity in our actions. We can humbly and honestly acknowledge our mistakes without the burden of shame, and use them for the wisdom and learning they can provide. The moment we open up to the vastness of who we are, we are awed and naturally become humble. Humility is a natural expression of our whole self because it allows us to see that although we are brilliant, fantastic, and loving, we can also be liars, cheaters, and incompetent. It allows us to be gentle and loving with ourselves regardless of what the circumstances of our external lives may be reflecting. Humility gives us the freedom to live authentically and stand with our higher power as we share our gifts with the world.

Signpost No. 4: Intolerance

It is the fear of our own flaws and the shame of our past experiences that make us intolerant of others. We are intolerant of those who reflect parts of ourselves that repel or frighten us. Intolerance has us harshly judge those who are different from us because we fear that accepting them will result in the admission of our own weaknesses. Superiority is the face of our intolerance, and this is its voice: "I am better than you, superior to you—in other words, more right than you." Feeling small and inadequate, we mistakenly believe that if we can somehow ignore these feelings and focus on other people's flaws, no one will find out the truth about who we are. Feeling imperfect or damaged, our wounded ego tries desperately to make itself bigger than it is by cutting others down, and it feeds on the sensation of righteousness that being intolerant provides. Left unchecked, the wounded ego will eventually construct an impenetrable fortress of righteous intolerance built on the condemnation and disdain we feel toward ourselves and others.

The intolerance we feel toward others is always a reflection of how intolerant we are of ourselves. Whenever we judge, hate, humiliate, or ostracize another, it is always because we fear being judged, humiliated, rejected, or stigmatized ourselves. If we were to give voice to what lies deeper than our intolerant thoughts and feelings, we would have to truthfully say, "Most of all, I fear being less than you."

Intolerance of ourselves or others without the balance of compassion turns into self-righteous rigidity, which cuts us off from our hearts and our conscience. It is one of the signposts for disaster because it breeds separateness, bigotry, and hate crimes. Intolerance in its most brutal form wants everything its way and will seek to eliminate anything that is different. Intolerance drives away loved ones, friends, and other important people, depriving us of companionship, connection, and love. Without our realizing it, our condemnation of others condemns us to a life of anger, bitterness, intolerance, and, very often, lonely desolation.

When our intolerant self is allowed to run rampant without the balance of compassion, it is just a matter of time before we end up wounding the very people we love the most. Believing that our view is the right view, we march forward oblivious to the feelings of others as we pass judgment on them.

Intolerance runs rampant in our society and shows itself in a myriad of ways. Criticizing and condemning the lifestyles of others is one expression of our intolerance. Impatience with the elderly or our children is a display of intolerance. Intolerance shows up in the act of cursing another driver on the road or feeling hatred for someone based on their sexual preference or political views. Condemning people for their religious beliefs—or lack thereof—is an all-too-common face of intolerance.

When we're being intolerant, we're presuming that we know what's right and what's wrong, what's good and what's bad, what's useful and what's not useful in any given situation—even if we have only limited information on which to base our opinions. This is a red flag! In the assumption that we know what's right, intolerance closes us off from seeing things in new ways, from going beyond the limitations of our past, and from finding new, more resourceful ways of relating to others. To the extent that we find ourselves being intolerant of people, ideas, and situations, we guarantee that our own lives will not change for the better. For when we take the adamant, resistive stance of intolerance, we are unable to step into any new thought, belief, or course of action that might threaten our righteous position and thus the status quo.

THE SPIRITUAL ANTIDOTE: COMPASSION

Our compassionate nature softens our intolerance with love and understanding, bringing into being the perfect balance. Compassion gifts us with patience, spaciousness, acceptance, tolerance, and love. When we are compassionate, our hearts feel big enough to accept others for who they are, including all their flaws. Compassion helps us recognize and come to terms with the fact that we, too, have flaws, make mistakes, and are at times confused, misguided, and uncertain. It allows us to see that it is our flaws and imperfections that give us our depth and our uniqueness. It allows us to look in the mirror and see our real beauty, even in the midst of our wounded ego's judgments and criticisms. Compassion gives us empathy and the license to be 100 percent ourselves. Through the spiritual eyes of compassion, we see ourselves as a precious child of this divine universe.

When our intolerance is balanced with compassion, we trust that every experience holds some wisdom and meaning, and we begin to view the painful incidents of our lives as opportunities to grow and discover a greater expression of ourselves. We can accept seemingly senseless events as being part of something of purpose, and we can find the beauty that is hidden from us when we are looking only through our limited individual perspective. Only when we temper our intolerance with compassion can we make peace with the person we've been and open up to the vastness of the person we can become.

Compassion is the antidote for our intolerance of others because it enables us to walk in another's shoes and imagine what it must be like to see life through their eyes. To invoke the spiritual antidote of compassion, we need only to breathe into our heart and say, "Let me see this situation from a broader perspective. Let me understand how this person or experience can serve the greater whole. Open me to the pain of another's heart." In the universal connection that compassion brings, we understand the pain and woundedness of others, so we're able to forgive those who have harmed us and are less tempted to take others' bad behavior personally. By enabling us to connect with the universal condition of human pain and suffering, compassion dissolves the illusion of separateness that keeps us in a perpetual role of victim or victimizer. With compassion we can move beyond the confines of our own resistance, beyond the shame and judgment that render us intolerant, and into the fullness of our true being. Compassion allows us to understand that, as citizens of the planet, we're all in this together and that in order to ensure our survival we must hold and cultivate a new and larger vision of what's possible for ourselves and for the human race as a whole.

One compassionate act can save someone's life. Just imagine for a moment that for every story of greed, lust, hate, intolerance, or selfishness that we are bombarded with on a daily basis, we heard one story of compassion: the father of two who didn't hesitate to risk life and limb to save another person from being killed by an oncoming subway car; the total stranger who lent a helping hand to a soul in pain, who unknowingly altered the course of that person's life; a random act of kindness that challenges someone's belief that no one cares and renews their faith in the goodness and connection of people. Compassion is a force as powerful as any act of hatred, but we must look for opportunities to express it.

Our compassionate nature holds the power to lift us beyond the veil of the small self and into the realm of the collective heart, where we have access to wisdom that is deeper than any illusion of separation. Connected to this wide-open field of love and awareness, we are naturally magnetic, drawing to us all that we need at the deepest level. Compassion is the great spiritual antidote to the intolerance that pervades the human condition.

Signpost No. 5: Self-Absorption

When our wounded ego is consumed with its own pain, loss, and limitations, we are more susceptible to being swept up by the swell of self-absorption. Becoming overly self-absorbed is a signpost of disaster because it's nearly impossible to see our own bad behavior and steer clear of potential pitfalls when we are myopically focused only on our small reality. When we are immersed only in our own joys and sorrows, trials and tribulations, we actually come to believe that our life is more important than the lives of those around us. Our good news is the only news that has to be shared, and our problems are the most painful, difficult, challenging—the hardest to solve. When we are only self-focused (or perhaps I should say "self-obsessed"), we easily become trapped in the "It's all about me" syndrome, which blinds us to the impact our behaviors have on other people.

Of course, it is our fear that we are not enough, that we are not important, and that we are nobody special that drives us to become self-absorbed. Our deep anxiety that we will be overlooked or that we won't be taken care of causes us to become consumed with our own needs and to obsessively seek attention. The experience of "not enough" breeds self-absorption as we compulsively try to get from the world what we fear we lack. Self-absorption is the culprit behind our increasingly rude society, where everyone seems to be crying out en masse, "What about me?"; "It's my turn!"; "I'm entitled to more time [or money, or attention, or things]!" When we are self-absorbed, we are rendered unconscious to anything outside our own personal needs and agendas. And because we are consumed with ourselves, we do not see the warning signs—the red flags—indicating that our choices and behaviors may be leading us in a dangerous direction.

Feelings of entitlement offer us a clue that we are headed down the path of self-absorption. When we believe that the world owes us something, our self-absorbed nature feels entitled to take whatever we want—be it an opportunity, another person's lover, or the chance to be at the center of attention. Our sense of entitlement has us believe that we are entitled to special treatment, regardless of the feelings of those around us. Self-absorption can blindside us if we are not aware of its dangers. The day may come when we are so consumed by our own needs that we find ourselves dipping into our children's trust fund or our company's expense account. Our self-absorbed behavior may have us feeling flush for the moment, but in the end it leaves us barren of others' love, respect, and friendship, and of our own dignity.

Self-absorption breeds narcissistic impulses and must be balanced by a genuine concern for the welfare of others and a commitment to contribute to making the world a better place. When we are focused only on ourselves, it is because we have lost sight of our connection to the greater whole. Contributing to others and giving something back is the only spiritual antidote that can balance out.

THE SPIRITUAL ANTIDOTE: BEING OF SERVICE

Our self-absorbed nature keeps us from accessing the aspect of ourselves that simply wants to make a difference in the world. This aspect, which exists at the core of every human being, is what makes this world the astonishing place that it is. When we are present to our contributory self, we know that we matter. We know that what we say and do is important, and we instinctively look out for the welfare of others as well as for our own. When we open up and are present to the part of us that yearns to be a part of the greater whole, we are suddenly transported beyond the smallness of the "me" factor and are able to balance our self-serving ways.

We are each born with an innate desire to contribute to and be a part of something greater than ourselves. It is our greatest honor and responsibility as human beings to serve others and when we are fully immersed in the grace of service, contributing to the world, and focused on giving instead of taking, we are gifted with a new perception—not only of the world and those in it, but of ourselves as well. By using our talents to their fullest—whether to raise money, lend a hand at a food line, or raise public awareness about one of the thousands of issues that are killing off our environment, our children, or our spirit—we are lifted out of the smallness of our individual problems and into a higher purpose. When we are willing to use our pain and misfortunes for the good of the greater whole, we are released from the bonds of our personal suffering.

Being of service requires us to release our expectations and attachment to what our contribution should look like and just allow ourselves to be used for the good of a greater whole. When our narcissistic impulses are balanced by our deeper desire to contribute to others, we become willing to make a higher choice—if not for ourselves, then for the sake of those we would serve. We're willing to feel the discomfort of not getting a personal need met when we see that our sacrifice may serve the needs of many. Being of service demands that we surrender our individual desires in favor of what is good for the collective whole. When we look from the perspective of how we can serve the greater whole, we search for ways to give back, to lend a hand—even if our ego's deepest, most secret desire is to amass wealth. Serving others is a divine gift that lifts us out of the painful cycle of being our worst enemy, because in serving others, we get to belong and be a contributing member of the collective heart.

Signpost No. 6: Stubbornness

We may think of stubbornness as a relatively harmless trait, but in our quest to understand the mechanisms of our own self-sabotage, we must expose the true cost of our rigid thinking and inflexibility. Stubbornness is essentially a form of unexpressed anger—or anger that has its heels dug in. Whenever another person threatens our autonomy or our power, whenever we sense that someone else is trying to guide us—or, God forbid, control us—our open and flexible nature begins to harden into a fixed rigidity. And when we lack the skills or the willingness to express our anger outright, to deal directly with whatever is challenging our authority, our unyielding, immovable anger turns back on itself and we find ourselves clinging tightly to our own perceptions, thoughts, and behaviors—whether they are useful or not.

Stubbornness might manifest itself as obnoxious self-righteousness, as quiet withdrawal, or as outright resistance against whomever or whatever we perceive to be our opponent. It's erected like a prison-yard fence that guards what we allow in and out of our own private reality. We pride ourselves on holding tightly to the righteous positions that we believe protect us from unwelcome and unwanted forces, but we sacrifice flexibility and openness in the process. Although at times it's appropriate to put our foot down when our boundaries are being tested, when stubbornness is not tempered with willingness, we find ourselves clinging to choices that don't serve us. Unwilling to view our opinions from a new perspective, we are blinded from seeing the destructive backlash of our resistant and unyielding stance.

Stubbornness is righteous anger that is cemented with fear and resistance. When we notice ourselves becoming too deeply invested in our own way of doing things, fighting too hard for the superiority of our own opinions, or closing ourselves off from the input of those around us, a red flag should go up in our awareness that alerts us that we are being used by the wounds of our egos. If this signpost of disaster is ignored, we will inevitably find ourselves quietly giving up much of what makes life worth living in the name of being "right." Our stubbornness has us decide that we would rather be right than be happy. We would rather be right than be loved. We would rather be right then be inconvenienced by change.

THE SPIRITUAL ANTIDOTE: WILLINGNESS

Willingness—to see another possibility, to consider a new perspective, and to admit that we do not have all the answers—is the spiritual antidote that melts the hardened position of stubbornness. When we are willing, we are open, movable, changeable, and malleable. No longer so deeply rooted in our own opinions, assumptions, and behaviors, we are open to feedback; we are able to grow in new ways and to open up to new opportunities that our stubbornness has held at bay.

With the spiritual antidote of willingness, we gain the strength to admit what we cannot change, what is out of our control, and what is not our business to begin with. Likewise, it's only when we are willing to accept the truth that we can see clearly what we *do* need to change and what *is* our responsibility. Willingness gives us the motivation to get into action, clean up our unfinished business, lay down our internal bats, and soften the stubborn positions of our wounded ego.

Stubbornness is nothing more than the tight grip of the wounded ego desperately trying to assert its power. For most of us, finding the willingness to loosen up, to let go of some control, and to allow things to unfold is not the easy road. It takes willingness to show up in life without our righteous beliefs, and yet this is the only path that leads to true intimacy, deep love, and fulfillment.

Consider for a moment what would be available to you if you allowed yourself to be more flexible, more malleable, more willing. What if you found the willingness to change the things that don't work for you and your life? What if you were willing to let go of the story you tell yourself about how people are and allowed them to show up differently? What if you were willing to be wrong about yourself, to question the dark thoughts, destructive impulses, and addictive behaviors that you've given your power to, and instead became willing to make choices that allow your highest expression to unfold?

Willingness is God's fertile ground; it's the stuff that reinvention is made of. With willingness we are able to radically reinvent ourselves and reevaluate our choices time and time again.

Signpost No. 7: Deceit

I once heard it said that the destiny of all liars is that they begin to believe their own lies. This is exactly what makes deceit so dangerous. Every act of fraud, extortion, tax evasion, addiction, or infidelity is infused with deceit. Addicts of all kinds are masters at hiding their behavior and lying to themselves and those around them about the damaging consequences of their behavior. Adulterers often start out telling themselves they are involved in a harmless flirtation, and deceive themselves about where their actions are leading them. The most adept con men are those who are able to manipulate the facts in such a way that it is difficult to untangle the truth from their fabrications. Extortionists are masters at the art of deception, twisting the facts while in the same breath accusing their victims of lying. Once you know what to look for, you can easily spot a deceitful person: he or she is usually the one questioning the integrity of others.

Deceit shows up in obvious as well as more subtle ways. We might tell people that we are happily married when we haven't had sex in a year. We might tell ourselves that our children are doing great even though they are stealing money from us and hanging out with the wrong people. We might rationalize that it's OK to cheat on our taxes or lie on our expense report because, after all, many people do. Whenever we catch ourselves lying, twisting the facts, fabricating stories, exaggerating, giving ourselves more credit than is due, or positioning ourselves in a way that does not reflect our true nature, we must recognize these behaviors as red flags calling our attention to our deceit. And if the deceit is allowed to continue without the sobering influence of honesty and integrity, it will eventually destroy our relationships, our health, our finances, or our careers.

We deceive ourselves and others because we don't want to face the pain of telling the truth. We don't want to go without or experience lack. We don't want to feel the discomfort of having a physical, psychological, or emotional need go unmet, so we turn our backs on our integrity and go down the road of deceit, hoping that we will feel better, get some instant gratification, look good, or be accepted. Deceiving others about our true nature affords us some opportunity that we fear we wouldn't get by telling the truth. The more we stretch the truth, the more we have to lie to keep up the charade, which is why one deceitful act leads to many others.

In the absence of integrity and honesty, our deceitful nature creates a haze of confusion around us that makes it difficult to keep our story straight or to remember which version of "the truth" we told to whom. As a result, we live in a state of paranoia, afraid that we may unknowingly divulge some piece of information that could contradict one of our lies. We begin to live in an increasingly small and secretive world where we have to exert a tremendous amount of energy just managing our deceitful acts. We live in the false hope that we will gain greater security, recognition, or love, but a life built on deceit amounts to a very shaky foundation that at any moment could cause our house of lies to come tumbling down. It's only a matter of time before we fail to cover our tracks and our secrets are exposed. And then everything that we never wanted to see or admit about ourselves smacks us in the face.

THE SPIRITUAL ANTIDOTE: INTEGRITY

Integrity is the antidote that balances our deceitful nature and gives us the courage to honestly evaluate whether our actions are consistent with our highest values. To offset the dangers of deceit, integrity has to start at home. Integrity is not an external status that we can claim, but a state of being that we must cultivate from within. Deceit urges us to hide our weaknesses, flaws, temptations, or dark urges, but integrity gives us the courage to embrace them as part of who we are and to see them in the broader context of our values and beliefs.

So often deceitful actions take place in the darkness of half awareness. We get caught up in a rush to the finish line or swept away by lust, greed, or intolerance. Integrity brings light to our dark impulses and forces us to be accountable for our actions. It helps us remember that our thoughts, words, and actions matter because we exist in relationship to a greater whole.

Every time we commit an act of deceit, it's because we're looking out only for ourselves. Integrity tempers our selfishness and helps us to remember the whole. It's more difficult to embezzle money from our company when we consider the lives of those who will be hurt by our actions. We would think twice before cheating on our spouses if we remembered who that person was for us when we took our vows. We wouldn't go to such great lengths to live a double life or feed our addictions if we were honest about the effects our behavior has on our parents, children, friends, lovers, and co-workers.

There can be no integrity without complete honesty. Pretending that telling a half truth is the same thing as being honest is just another way to deceive ourselves. Integrity loses the battle with deceit whether we've stolen a thousand dollars or a hundred thousand, or whether we cheated on our spouse one night or have carried on a clandestine affair for years.

Having integrity requires us to come into balance with each area of our lives and make peace with ourselves as well as our past. When we live our lives from a place of integrity, we are able to stand tall, be transparent, be seen, and be exposed. We don't feel the need to hide who we are or what we are doing, and we feel safe having others view our daily habits. When our deceitful nature is balanced by integrity, we have the confidence to open the doors to our homes, our businesses, our bank accounts, and our credit reports and feel proud that we are responsible, contributing members of our communities. It keeps us on the straight road to success—the path that ensures that we will uphold our values, remember what is important, and make conscious choices.

If we're living a life of integrity, we don't have to worry about the other signposts. When we're being honest with ourselves and true to our values, we will admit it when we're being greedy, guarded, intolerant, stubborn, self-absorbed, or deceitful and get the help we need. Integrity leaves us a trail to follow when we've lost touch with our higher self. Where deceit guarantees a life of fear, shame, and uncertainty, the spiritual antidote of integrity delivers peace of mind and a joyous heart.

11

THE STRENGTH OF
FORGIVENESS

Forgiveness is the hallway between the past and the future, between our small, individual self and the all-inclusive nature of our highest self. Forgiveness is the holy medicine of the unhealed heart. It is the magical elixir that ensures life beyond our automatic human programming. It is the only door into a pain-free future. From its emotionally and spiritually fertile soil, forgiveness bears exorbitant amounts of love, health, peace, vitality, intimacy, and success.

Many years ago, someone gave me a card that read "Love is the answer—whatever the question." Ultimately, I believe that love *is* the answer, the healing balm, the spiritual solution that holds the power to end the war that rages within each of us and heal the split that separates us from our divine nature. When we feel loved and loving, we naturally make choices that are in the highest and best interest of all concerned. But before we can experience the pure and serene state of love, there is one priceless gift we must learn how to give—to ourselves and to others. If we are willing to give this gift, we are guaranteed a life of deepening wisdom, gratitude, expansion, and evolution. If we withhold this gift from ourselves or others, we are guaranteed a life of pain, misfortune, and excruciating repetition. The gift I am speaking of is *forgiveness*.

To heal the split between our dark side and our higher self, we must learn how to forgive ourselves for our imperfections, for our conflicting desires, for our unhealthy urges, for our judgmental minds, and for our cynical thoughts. We have to make peace with the aspects of ourselves and our lives that we have ignored, neglected, abused, violated, betrayed, and hated—even in the subtlest of ways. We must forgive ourselves for all of our personal agendas and our righteous positions that have led us to believe that we are better than, less than, and separate from others.

We also must find the willingness to forgive those who have hurt us, lied to us, disappointed us, and betrayed us, because only then will we put a stop to the crippling resentments, battles, and ego struggles that siphon off our life force. Ultimately, we have to learn how to forgive the presence that we think of as God, whether we call it Spirit, the Divine, Source, or by any other name. We have to admit that we are, in fact, angry at this presence, which I will refer to as God. We have to be willing to feel the heartbreak of having suffered through disappointments, addictions, health crises, molestation, or physical violence, and forgive our creator for allowing us to be born into a world where these things can happen.

To the wounded ego, forgiving is the same as admitting defeat. From the wounded ego's limited perspective, true relief and restitution can come only from engaging in blame, hate, and revenge. Our small self hangs on for dear life to our self-righteousness and our rage, and these become our consolation prize. The pain that we carry as a result of the wrongs that we feel others have perpetrated against us becomes part of our identity, and we find a kind of sick comfort in marinating in our misery. For some of us, being miserable feels better than forgiving and initiating a positive change in our lives. We resist releasing our pain because we don't want to give up our victim badge. For many of us it is the only thing we have left to hold on to. What has us resist forgiveness is the false belief that we will have to let someone (or worse yet, ourselves) off the hook, or that we are being asked to forget the painful events that have happened in our lives. Our wounded ego would rather go down with the ship than step into the life raft of forgiveness.

But until we forgive, we will continue to punish ourselves. Self-destruction and self-sabotage—whether we're consciously perpetrating it or whether we just find ourselves inexplicably, unwittingly drawn to it—are a form of self-punishment. Have you ever heard the saying "The guilty seek punishment"? The guilt we feel about our misdeeds gets registered in our conscience whether we like it or not. Most of us are experts at pretending that the bad things we do don't matter, and that's why we continue to repeat bad patterns. But truth be told, every time we do something that hurts ourselves or another, we register it in our psyches (tallying up our violations), and then we attract an unfortunate event in order to try to balance out and relieve ourselves of our guilt and shame. Here's a story that illustrates this perfectly. It happened recently to a friend of mine who is a hypnotherapist.

Stephanie was working with a client whom she knew was engaged in illegal deeds. After her session with him, he peeled $150 from his wad of cash and looked her in the eyes, saying, "I know you'll take this dirty money." As if in a trance, Stephanie took the money, even though she had a sick feeling in her stomach, and then left her office to visit a friend. Hours later, when she came out of her friend's house to drive home, her car was nowhere to be found. After a few minutes of panicking, believing that her car had been stolen, she was assured by her friend that her car was illegally parked and that more than likely it had been towed away. Annoyed, Stephanie asked her friend to help her see if she could find her car. On the way to the towing area it suddenly dawned on Stephanie that the money she would have to pay to get her car back would probably equal the amount of "dirty money" she had taken. And of course, this is exactly what happened: the amount of the towing fee combined with the ticket on the windshield exactly equaled the amount she had accepted from her client. She told me she actually felt relieved this had happened because she didn't feel right about taking the money in the first place and somehow the punishment she received in the outer world relieved the burden of her "crime."

Most of us are walking around carrying a huge and heavy load of guilt on our conscience. We feel guilty for not measuring up to our ego's ideals, ashamed of the desperate things we have done to win love and recognition and of the ways we have used the outer world to meet our inner needs. We feel bad about the choices we've made out of ignorance, vengeance, or instant gratification, and remorseful for our overindulgences and reckless behaviors. Most of us bury this pain and just keep on going, never taking the time to acknowledge or digest it. We feel that we need to move faster and faster, trying to outrun the day our pain will eventually catch up with us. It's as if our shadow is actually chasing us—and it is.

Then on top of this growing mass of guilt, fear, and shame we paint a nice bright smile, construct a more acceptable facade, and do our best to pretend that the things that are eating us up inside don't really bother us all that much. Ironically, self-sabotage is nothing more than a diversion that keeps us from coming face-to-face with all of the pain we've been stuffing inside—the traumas we haven't known how to deal with, the embarrassment that threatened our egos, and the shame that continues to erode our self-esteem. When we are desperate to protect ourselves from confronting what feels like a bottomless well of our own inner pain, good people are capable of and driven to do all sorts of bad things.

But here is where we can observe the absolute genius of the universe at work: Human beings were designed to be self-punishing creatures. Even if we succeed at blocking our shame from our conscious awareness—even if we minimize it, rationalize it, or pretend it doesn't exist—deep inside, we know the score. We know when we have violated someone else and when we have allowed ourselves to be violated. We know when we have cheated and when someone has cheated us. We know in the silent chambers of our own inner world when we are living as less than the person we are capable of being. So, as a way to punish ourselves, we enact quiet acts of self-sabotage or flagrant acts of self-destruction as a way to open the wound, because instinctively we know that this is the only way it can heal.

Continuing to beat ourselves up for being imperfect and for the misdeeds of our past is not a road that will lead to happiness or wholeness. The internal bat that we use against ourselves only keeps us trapped in a perpetual cycle of shame, violation, and self-abuse. It's easy to minimize the impact that our own self-hatred has on us, because much of it takes place in the privacy of our own minds, concealed from the world (or so we think). But it is vital that we grasp the damage that we do to ourselves every time we badger ourselves for our mistakes and imperfections. A couple of years ago I was thinking about how I could get the people who come to my retreats to see the severity of their self-abuse and the consequences that their self-abuse has on them. I finally came up with a way to demonstrate both its severity and its consequences that seems to really drive the message home.

The most powerful workshop I lead is a three-day retreat I call the Shadow Process. On the third day of the process, I bring a beautiful little baby doll to the front of the seminar room, one with an innocent face and pretty rosy cheeks; you may have had one just like it when you were a child. I hold it up and show it to everybody in the room and ask them to imagine that it represents a young, innocent version of themselves that still exists inside them. Then I take this adorable little baby doll and put her in my chair so we can all coo over her for a minute. Then, without warning, I pick the baby doll up, look at her sternly, and say, *"Why did you do that? You're a stupid idiot. What is wrong with you? You shouldn't have said that!"*

As I'm battering her with my verbal abuse, I take the little baby doll and give her a couple of good whacks across the top of my chair. Meanwhile, everybody in the room is hysterically laughing, because they all know exactly what I'm talking about. *"God, you're ugly. You really look like crap,"* I tell her. *"You should take better care of yourself. Nobody's ever going to love you. You're a fat pig. You shouldn't be so selfish. Why can't you do anything right? What's wrong with you? You're a bitch. You really blew it this time. You're such a loser. Nobody wants to be your friend."* I keep screaming at the baby doll, whacking it harder and harder across the top of my chair until an arm inevitably flies off and its pretty little head is left hanging on by only a string.

Then I take the baby, whose limbs have fallen off and whose head is slumped against its chest, and I do my best to prop it back up on my chair. I pat it on the head and say to it in my nicest, most spiritual voice, "Go out and have a great day, honey. Create a great life. Go make friends. Go make some money. You can do it. You can be anything you want to be, little baby. The world is yours. Just think it, and you can create it." But unfortunately, having been racked by my ceaseless abuse, my baby doll doesn't look like she's up for doing much of anything.

The point is that our self-abuse has an impact. Each time we criticize ourselves, neglect ourselves, and berate ourselves for our faults and our mistakes, we are beating ourselves up. We *are* that baby. We may be all grown up, but underneath we are still that innocent child who wanted to be good, to please others, to receive love, to matter, to make a difference, and to have a great life.

We didn't decide at the age of two or three that we were going to grow up and be miserable and angry. We didn't choose to become out-of-control, self-destructive addicts. We didn't decide to be criminals who victimize other people. We didn't consciously set out to become victims who get abused over and over again by ourselves and others. These things happened as a result of our toxic shame and the abuse—self-inflicted and otherwise—that we allowed into our lives because we thought we deserved it. These things happened as a result of the separation from our true essence.

Every wounding incident holds the potential to be a catalyst that will mend the separation between our lower self and our higher self. But if we don't make amends for the things we feel bad about, if we don't start treating ourselves with the love, care, and attention we so desperately need, the sad reality is that we probably will in fact continue to be our own worst enemies.

Making Amends

We will not be able to forgive ourselves for the crimes we've committed until we make amends for the things we've done to others that we feel bad about. We have to take responsibility for our behaviors and clean up the wreckage we've left in our path. It always amazes me that even if we know that making amends will allow us to feel good about ourselves and free us from the mistakes of our past, so many of us will not do it because of our own false pride. Our false pride tells us, "What's done is done. They won't get it anyway. There is nothing I can do about it now"; or "I did something so horrible I could never be forgiven." Our false pride heeds all the warnings of why making amends is not a good idea and convinces us there is no way to make our wrongs right. But this just isn't true. There is always a way to right the wrongs of our past, and it's our job to figure out how.

Recently, a gentleman named Ricardo attended the Shadow Process retreat. He had stolen hundreds of thousands of dollars from his family's business. He knew he would be written out of his parents' will and shunned from the family forever if he admitted to his fraud. He was convinced he was doomed, and because of this belief he kept creating circumstances in his life and his other businesses that reminded him monthly of what a bad guy and horrible son he had become. So when it came time for the forgiveness part of the process, he was stuck. I had to sit down with him to help him to see how he could clear his conscience so that he could go on with his life and live in peace. Not only was the guilt he felt about his actions affecting his business; it was destroying his relationship with his wife and keeping him from being present with his kids.

It took some time and an enormous amount of attention to get him to see that he could indeed slowly return a little of the money he still had left to his family's estate (even though he had gambled away most of it) and that he could spend ten days a year building homes and raising funds for a nonprofit in his area that does great work in housing orphaned children—all as a way of repaying the debt. Ricardo realized he would have to give back to his family in other ways. He made a commitment to support them and listen to them when they needed his ear and to help out his handicapped sister one day a week. Thus he could begin to relieve himself of the shameful guilt he carried into his every relationship and business deal. When Ricardo finally finished making amends for the crimes of his past, a spark of light came through his eyes, and you could actually see and feel the shift he experienced inside.

Why is this? It is because ultimately we are the judge and the jury for our own lives. We are the ones who have to come to terms with, and make the choice to forgive ourselves for, the crimes we have committed against others and ourselves. Our other heartbreaking choice is to continue the cycle of abuse, passing it down from generation to generation, letting our own guilt spill over into our friendships, our bodies, our finances, our businesses, and our future relationships. The guilty seek punishment, and there is no way to cover up this fact. It is a mechanism built into our human hard wiring, and if we accept this truth we can snap out of our own denial, confront our shame and guilt straight on, and do what we need to do to feel great inside ourselves. It's not always easy to see how taking an action in the present moment to clean something up from the past will support us in feeling better about our lives, but this outcome I guarantee. In fact, if this is all each of us did, we would radically shift our relationship with ourselves, others, and the world.

There are no shortcuts to this process. You may just want to close this book and forget about even trying to absolve yourself of your guilt and bad feelings, because the thought seems too overwhelming. But before you do, let me point out to you a few of the benefits and rewards you can look forward to if you have the courage to forge ahead.

A peaceful mind

Feelings of worthiness

Inspiration

The ability to hear the voice of your higher self

Self-respect

Self-esteem

The desire to be around people who love and respect you

More passion for life

More hope for the future

A deeper connection with those around you

More intimacy

A sense of dignity

A feeling of accomplishment

The freedom to move forward with your life

An innate feeling of well-being

Liberation of your heart and mind

A sense of completion with the past

Authentic pride

Joy

Ultimately, forgiveness is the only antidote for our self-abuse and our abuse of others. If we do not take the courageous step into forgiveness, we are guaranteed to repeat the painful mistakes of our past, and they will more than likely continue to get more painful. We are guaranteed to create blocks to our successes and to fall into the same holes by the side of the road. We will continue to create and be drawn to negative experiences that will remind us of the guilt, shame, and self-loathing we have accumulated within our psyches. Every time we create a so-called bad experience, we can use it as further confirmation that we are bad, unworthy, and flawed, or we can view it as an indicator that there is more internal work to be done. In other words, there is more that we need to forgive.

The Peace Treaty

It is an act of forgiveness to compassionately acknowledge that we have made mistakes and have done things that were emotionally and sometimes physically wounding to ourselves and others. It is an act of forgiveness to make amends and then let go of the grudges, resentments, and blame we are still harboring toward ourselves or another. True forgiveness demands that we stop beating ourselves up for our mistakes and imperfections and cultivate compassionate self-love instead. It replaces hate, judgment, and condemnation with love, acceptance, and understanding. Forgiveness purifies our hearts, cleans the slate, and supports us in creating a life we love and in building the kinds of relationships we've always desired.

Although forgiveness often looks like a generous gift we are giving to someone else, it is ultimately an act of self-love and a gift we give to ourselves. Only through forgiveness can we take back our power and move on with our lives. When we forgive, we break free from the bondage of our resentments and are released from the prison of our past. Forgiveness opens the door to greater intimacy, compassion for ourselves and others, and new hope for the future. It creates the space in our emotional world that is necessary for us to experience more love, joy, peace, and freedom. Forgiveness allows us to let go of the burdens of the past in favor of having full access to the magnificence of who we are now and who we can become.

There is nothing—and I mean nothing—that will give you more of what you want and need in life than forgiveness. Forgiving yourself, others, God, and the world is the only measure powerful enough to end the internal war. Forgiveness leads to peace.

In his book *Gandhi: An Autobiography,* Gandhi said, "Hate the sin; love the sinner." This is a crucial distinction for us to understand if we are going to transcend our self-hatred, release our resentments, give up our grudges, and move into forgiveness.

We must understand that we have all sinned and others have sinned against us and that if we hate the sinner (ourselves or another), we only perpetuate the cycle of abuse. If we can distinguish the sin, the act or behavior, from the sinner, we can begin the process of healing our hearts and moving into higher realms of consciousness where we will find peace, contentment, and fulfillment.

Forgiving Others

My favorite spiritual teacher, Emmet Fox, once said, "Our resentments bind us to the person with a cord stronger than steel." Now, would you want to be bound, by a cord stronger than steel, to the person who has hurt you, betrayed you, lied to you, or screwed you over? How stupid would that be? First they rip part of your heart out, and then you give them the rest of it! By clinging to your resentments, you rob yourself of your power, your peace of mind, and your ability to create yourself anew. It makes no sense. And just in case you think you are actually hurting the person who wronged you by holding on to your grudges and resentments, let me clue you in. Most of them *don't care* if you are hurt and angry. It's no skin off their back. In fact, some of the people you are devoting your thoughts, feelings, and precious energy to hating are now dead. So now not only do you not have access to all of your power, but you have buried it alive in someone else's grave. Crazy, right?

We hold on to our resentments only when we are still trying to prove that we are right and someone else is wrong. Maybe we're still struggling to change what happened in the past or trying to regain a sense of control over our present circumstances. Maybe we still love the person who hurt us, so we would rather be connected to them in a negative way than not to be connected at all. Or maybe they have now become our excuse for why we are not living the life we want to live, for why we are stuck, or for why we continue to beat ourselves up. These are just a few of the reasons we hold on to our resentments. But no matter what the reason, if we want to move on, to have a life greater than the one we have right now in this moment, we must forgive.

I've personally been through so many difficult times in my life. Some were definitely self-induced, and some were probably karmic—in other words, unavoidable or meant to be. But no matter how they came about, or whose fault they were, whether I created them or co-created them, whether I believe myself to be the victim or the victimizer, I've gone through many difficult situations. They are over now, and it no longer matters who was right or who was wrong, what they did or what I did. The only thing that matters is whether I can see the consequences of my actions or inactions and whether I've learned the lessons that these experiences have tried to bestow upon me. There are a few questions that I always try to spend a sufficient amount of time dwelling on when I'm trying to find the gifts that ultimately lead me to forgiveness.

- How can I use this experience to become the kind of person my soul longs to be?

- How can I use this lesson so that others can learn from me and maybe bypass a difficult life experience?

- How can I use this incident to heal my own heart?

- How can I use this lesson to help the healing of the planet?

Believe me, when I am angry or hurt, the last thing I want to do is ask these questions. Hurt and anger leave me feeling righteous and shut down. So first I have to give myself permission to feel, be with, and accept all the anger and hurt I'm carrying. I have to get out of my head, where I can justify and rationalize all my pain, and get into the heart of my inner child—the little, sensitive part of me that has learned to hold on to pain as a form of self-protection. I have to, with open arms, give myself all the internal space I need to do the kind of healing work necessary to let go of the past, to forgive myself, and to forgive others. I have to acknowledge the aspect of myself that would rather hang on for dear life to my story, my position, my evidence, and my reasons rather than take responsibility and give up the blame.

And just to be clear: We don't forgive for the sake of the other person. We forgive for the sake of ourselves. We do it for our freedom. You may have heard the Buddhist saying, "Holding on to anger is like grasping a hot coal with the intent of throwing it at someone else, but ultimately, you are the one who gets burned." The anger, resentment, and rage that we hold toward others robs us of seeing thousands of great possibilities that are right in front of our eyes. Our resentments give others our power, our precious life force, and the ability to take away our peace and our happiness. I recommend you take it all back. Forgive.

The moment we are willing to let go, we fertilize the ground of our consciousness—a necessity if we are to continue to grow and move forward. We must till the soil of our psyches and root out the dead and useless emotional weeds so that we can prepare ourselves for a new and exciting future.

When we take on the process of forgiveness from the perspective of our wounded egos, it can easily become an intellectual endeavor. If we feel guilty or are uncomfortable with our anger or resentments, we may try to "skip steps" in our healing process by "spiritualizing" our suffering. We may say things like "It was meant to be" or "It's all in God's plan," when that couldn't be farther from the truth of how we feel. Forgiveness demands that we plant our feet firmly in reality once and for all by accepting the past, which we have no power to change—and take responsibility for our own behavior, which we do have the power to change. It is only when we can accept the past exactly as it is that we can experience true forgiveness, because only from that space are we able to extract the wisdom of our experiences and find the gifts hidden within our pain. Finding the gifts of our past requires us to step outside our wounded, victimized self and see with the eyes of our highest self. From the higher perspective, we can trust that things are exactly as they should be and that the universe is conspiring with us to provide us exactly those experiences that we need to grow and evolve.

Note that forgiveness does not ask us to agree with, condone, or tolerate bad behavior. In fact, by forgiving, we give ourselves permission to move beyond bad behavior by learning the lessons and extracting the wisdom from these experiences. Forgiving others does not mean we will become wimps, pushovers, or easy marks for the predators of the world. It doesn't mean we won't take steps to protect ourselves in healthy ways or set clear and strong boundaries with those who would continue to try to victimize us. Far from it; forgiveness allows us to step out of the role of victim and into our power, to see situations and circumstances clearly and take whatever actions are necessary to ensure that we don't make the same mistakes again.

The voice of forgiveness says, "It's time to move on"; "I accept the past"; and "This experience helped me become a wiser and more compassionate person." Forgiveness encourages us to release the need to have our past be any different than it was. At the same time it requires us to give up the grievances we hold against ourselves and the world so that we are no longer held prisoner by the gravitational pull of the past. It's impossible to soar in life, to express ourselves, and to share our greatest gifts if we are weighed down by the pain and suffering of years' worth of resentments, anger, and blame. Through forgiveness we are able to look the past squarely in the eye and then compassionately let it go so that we may move forward unencumbered.

Forgiveness unfolds once we understand that everything that has happened to us happened for a reason. The moment we can see the blessings of what we have received, the wisdom that we now hold, and the skills that we now possess because of painful or traumatic circumstances, we naturally forgive. Then the pain in our hearts is transformed into gratitude, and the confusion in our minds is replaced with clarity. Forgiving others is evidence that we love ourselves enough to be able to say good-bye, to move on, to leave the past in the past. When we find the courage to cut the cords that negatively bind us to others, that strip us of self-esteem, we take back our power; we see ourselves as bigger than our resentments and more powerful than our heartaches.

We receive many gifts when we choose the bold and courageous act of forgiveness. Most of all, we are free. As *A Course in Miracles,* one of the most spiritual texts ever written, states: "The holiest of all the spots on earth is where an ancient hatred becomes a present love." Forgiveness challenges us to find the gold in the dark, the wisdom in our wounds, and the possibility hidden within our pain.

Forgiving God

I must have embraced the fact that I am a whistle-blower, because here I am being one again. Although most of us won't admit it, I believe that many of us are angry at the Universe, at whomever we believe to be our creator. We are angry at God. If you think about it, this is easy to understand. What good is a God who is supposed to be there for you, to answer your prayers, to protect you, to take care of you in times of distress, and who then appears not to show up? We've been disappointed. We've been let down. Many of us prayed to God to be there for us, to take away our pain, and to protect us from the abuse that we incurred or witnessed as children. We believe that if God was on our side, God would have been there to shield us from bad things in the first place. But this is one of the hard, cold facts of life: God can't protect us from evil. Some things are simply meant to happen in order for our souls to grow and evolve. We need to have human experiences—including experiences of heartache and pain—in order to open up to the highest expression of ourselves. Like a beautiful pearl that is formed, layer upon layer, in response to an ongoing invasion of shells and sand, we, too, are shaped by the irritants and suffering we endure. The pain of our human experiences—when purified through forgiveness—provides us with wisdom and transforms us into a thing of great beauty.

When we don't look from a broader perspective at the wisdom of our human experiences, we naturally get angry at God. When we see all the suffering, all those who have been hurt, whose lives have been destroyed, whose homes or security have been taken away, it's easy to get angry at the one power that we believe should save us from these hardships. I want to tell you that this anger is OK. You don't have to hide it anymore. You don't have to beat yourself up over it. You don't have to pretend it's not there. In fact, acknowledging your anger toward God is one of the first steps of forgiveness.

I was blessed to be present for an eye-opening experience of what happens when people allow themselves to acknowledge (that's the hardest part), express, and release their anger at God. Several years ago, I had the honor of leading a three-day intensive workshop with my good friend Neale Donald Walsch, the author of the Conversations with God series. Neale loves to talk, so he did most of the talking, and I led most of the processes.

We were the perfect match. The room we had rented for the weekend was in an old church in downtown La Jolla, California. We had brought our own sound system with us to ensure that we would have the music and the acoustics to deliver a powerful experience for those who participated and that, when powerful music was being played, the attendees would feel uninhibited enough to let themselves participate freely.

On the second night of the workshop I decided to lead the group in an anger process that was specifically focused on the anger that people were holding toward God. There were a little over a hundred people in the room, and we gave each person plenty of room and a blindfold so they could do the exercise safely and without feeling self-conscious about being watched by others. One crucial part of the anger process is the style and progression of music that we play. It's in four distinct stages of intensity; we play it very loudly, and it helps everybody mobilize the energy of all their unprocessed rage.

Neale had already done a great job of introducing what we were going to do, including giving everybody permission to be angry at God, at least for the evening. I then took them through an internal process to open them up to all the times they thought God should have been there for them and wasn't and all the times their prayers seemed to go unanswered. I asked them to get in touch with all the deep disappointment they harbored about the way their lives had turned out, and to unearth the shame they felt about being angry at God.

By the time we were ready to start the process, they were pretty pissed off. So we started the music. I was speaking loudly into the microphone. People were already doing some deep breathing. But at the moment when it was time for people to let out their anger in words and screams, to voice their rage aloud—the music suddenly stopped. This was actually my worst nightmare, because the music is so important to the process, and I half-expected people to come out of the process when the music stopped.

Instead, for the next twenty minutes this group of more than a hundred screamed so loudly—crying, yelling, admonishing, and spewing their pent-up anger toward God—that nobody even noticed that the music had stopped. The cries of pain and rage were so loud that you wouldn't have been able to hear the music anyway. In all the years I've been leading workshops, I have never witnessed such a powerful release of suppressed rage—rage that participants didn't even know they were harboring.

Acknowledging our anger is an important step. We have to acknowledge all the times we have reached out in need or desperation and felt that God was not there. We have to feel the helplessness we felt when we were in the middle of some horrible situation that we believed God should resolve.

A few years ago I found out that someone had been continually lying to me in the midst of a business deal that wound up costing me thousands of dollars and hundreds of hours of my time. At the time, I felt like I was working very hard to make this world a better place, and I became enraged that God, or my higher self, would let this happen to me. It took me months and months of reliving the various scenarios between myself and this person to figure out that this ever-loving presence had tried countless times to warn me. Many people had told me to watch my back with this person, but I wanted him to like me, so I chose to ignore the warnings. I chose to do what my mind wanted instead of tuning in to, and having faith in, the messages coming to me. I paid for this in ways that I cannot even describe. It took me a few years to admit that at the time I had stopped relying on God for my guidance because I was angry at God for all the times I felt let down, betrayed, or abandoned in my life. Unknowingly, I had lost my faith without even realizing it.

To forgive God, we have to admit to our faithlessness and the extent to which our anger and disappointment have cut us off from our own source. Only after we have vented our rage can we begin to see the ways in which God does, in fact, work in our lives. When we've cracked the hard shell of our anger, we can begin to see the things that God has been trying to show us all along. We can look through divine eyes rather than through the eyes of our small, individual, wounded self.

Forgiveness gives us the understanding that it is not God's job to save us from all the evil or pain that we will encounter, because these things are part of our human experience. As soon as we find the courage to face and accept things as they are, and not as we would like them to be, we become present to the things we can and must change.

Patrick had been a victim of a woman who was living with a secret addiction. Although he was devastated and angry that she was able to pull the wool over his eyes, in the end his real resentment and rage were focused on her family, who had known about her addiction and kept it a secret from him. When I was taking Patrick through the forgiveness process with the intention of helping him in letting go of the resentments he held toward her family, what unexpectedly emerged was his deeper resentment toward God.

In a moment of clarity, Patrick saw that the reason he couldn't forgive the family, although he had tried for years, was that it really wasn't them he was still blaming. Patrick understood their deceit and dysfunctional allegiance. Surprised, he discovered that he was really angry at the God he believed should and would have protected him from these kinds of horrible injustices. In this process, Patrick realized there was a very innocent part of him that believed that if he loved God he would love him in return and protect him through thick and thin. I supported him in allowing his anger to emerge without judgment or condemnation. He was able to feel it and admit to it; he was then able to see all the ways that God had tried to warn him: impulses, instincts, moments of awareness, little knots in his stomach—all God's ways of trying to get his attention. Retrospectively he could see the signs and warnings that he had ignored. Once he was able to understand that he would grow and evolve from this devastating experience, he was able to forgive God, the family, and himself.

The moment we release our resentment toward God, we are once again able to recognize the signs that are all around us— our instincts, hunches, inner urges, and outer roadblocks. We can recognize the voice of God like a nudge from a good friend who gently points us in the right direction but loves us enough to allow us to make our own choice.

When you forgive the force that you think of as God, you are suddenly able to see a reality beyond your narrow human perspective and understand that everything that has happened to you is ultimately serving you in becoming the grandest, greatest version of yourself. Aligned with the force you know as God, you feel yourself as a powerful co-creator of your life and open up to allowing your life to be used for the good of all. You return to your God-given, natural state of innocence.

Forgiveness of Self

Self-forgiveness means absolving ourselves of any sort of blame, resentment, or recrimination that we've used to beat ourselves up. As children, most of us got in trouble even when we didn't do anything wrong, and we made the unconscious decision that it was *our* fault. We were innocent "victims" (so to speak) who then went on to blame ourselves, hence becoming the victimizers. We picked up the victimizer's bat, blurred the lines between what is "our stuff" and what is "their stuff," and were never able to distinguish those boundaries again. We were the ones who took responsibility for things we didn't even do, and then we used those things to beat ourselves up, over and over again. How many times have I heard people coming to me five, ten, twenty, and forty years later, beating themselves up for things they didn't do or had no control over—other people's bad behavior. We beat ourselves up for being molested; for being raped; for being left, cheated on, betrayed, lied to; for being defrauded. It's bad enough that we beat ourselves up for things that we participate in, but then we add insult to injury by taking on the crimes of others. Sue is a perfect example of a woman who was taking responsibility for crimes committed against her.

For six years, Sue was emotionally beaten up by her husband day in and day out. She finally left him, but a year later she was still in excruciating emotional pain, and her daily suffering led her to start praying for forgiveness and for the ability to see the truth so she could let go and move on. For three of those six years her life and livelihood were threatened, but because she didn't have any physical scars, she didn't realize how badly abused she truly was. So instead she took all the responsibility for the breakdown of her marriage and continued beating herself up emotionally for wrecking her family and leaving her husband. Then one day as she was going to get something from her car, she opened the door, and the tip of the window just happened to hit her arm in a place that broke a blood vessel. Within minutes she had a six-inch black and blue bruise that made it look like someone had taken a bat and beaten her. By the next day the ugly bruise had spread over her whole bicep. It was not until she saw the externalization of this huge black and blue mark that it dawned on her that her husband had been doing just this: he hit her daily, over and over again, with his teasing, his belittling comments, his twisting of events and facts, and his shaming of her for her big heart and all her accomplishments. He beat her with threats, domination, and control. But since it was emotional and psychological abuse, she couldn't see it: all of her bruises were inside. The bruises were all over her but hidden. In an instant she woke up from the trance and saw that she had been a battered woman and that she was now battering herself.

Sue was one of many victims of an often unrecognized form of abuse called *psychological warfare*. Even though living with the abuse led her to getting a divorce, because of her sweet nature and her forgiving heart she more often than not went back into denying that he was really that bad and instead mercilessly tortured herself and convinced herself that she was bad and wrong and therefore the victimizer. However, now this large bruise that she carried around for two weeks became the undeniable and shocking visible proof that she was really the victim. Sue needed to begin the process of self-forgiveness and to say to herself that she was sorry for putting herself in this horri-bly abusive relationship, for staying in it even though she had been given many warnings to get out earlier, and then for using the abuse she endured to beat herself up. Self-forgiveness is a heart-opening process that begins the moment we tell the truth and become compassionate and humble enough to say we're sorry for all the ways we've knowingly or unknowingly hurt oth-ers or ourselves.

Just as we have to separate the sin from the sinner in order to forgive those who have perpetrated acts of neglect, deceit, or abuse against us, we must now separate ourselves from the acts we have committed against others and ourselves. Now, let me wake you up to the facts, just in case you have slipped into de-nial. We have all done things to hurt other people. We have all failed to live up to the expectations of others, spoken words that pierced others' wounds, overstepped people's boundaries, sto-len, lied, deceived, gossiped, enabled, withheld the truth, gone into drunken stupors, and shamed those who are close to us. We have all made promises we didn't keep, flirted with people other than our spouses, or wished someone harm inside our own minds. We have screamed at our children, rejected someone who was deeply in love with us, or avoided paying our taxes. We are all sinners in some regard, and although our crimes might not seem as terrible as our neighbor's or as those of the people featured on last night's news, we still have to realize the cost of the grudges we hold against ourselves. We have to learn to separate our actions from who we are as people. If we don't, we will have to suffer the consequences of living as a beaten-down version of ourselves.

Forgiveness means laying down the internal bats that we use to beat ourselves up. It means letting go of all of the self-induced, torturous internal messages that we replay over and over again in our minds and choosing peace instead of heartache, gratitude instead of guilt, solitude instead of noise, and love instead of war. It means forgiving ourselves for all the people we have hurt—both directly and indirectly—and for the acts of violence we have committed against our own bodies, minds, and psyches. It means forgiving ourselves for the mistakes we've made, for holding ourselves to unrealistic expectations and standards, and for not being perfect—in other words, for being human. Forgiveness requires us to internally make amends and then forgive ourselves for the nasty and sometimes horrible things we have done to other people.

You can start by telling the sweet, innocent child who lives within you that you are sorry for all the times you made poor choices, disregarded your better judgment, and put yourself in harm's way. You can tell yourself you're sorry for all the times you took things that were not rightfully yours and for the ways you bullied, harassed, or beat up on others. Ask yourself for forgiveness for all the times you participated in behaviors that hurt those you love, for the times you didn't have faith and allowed fear to guide your actions. And, just as important, you must forgive yourself for all the times you sold your soul and violated your own boundaries in order to gain the love, respect, or approval of others. You begin the process of forgiveness when you acknowledge all the times you have made reactive choices in an attempt not to be inconvenienced or to avoid feeling the pain of right action.

Forgiveness is about healing your emotional self and dissolving the shame that you carry. It is a personal dialogue between you and the most private, delicate parts of yourself—an intimate conversation written for you and by you. This is where the healing needs to take place. When we forgive ourselves, we take back all the energy we have put into others and redirect it into our own tender hearts. I'm going to assert that self-forgiveness is the only guaranteed path to giving ourselves the love and compassion we deserve. When we let go of the regrets and resentments from the past, we become present to the radiant jewel that we are—a multifaceted gem whose flaws contribute to its unique beauty.

Just breathe into that: *you are a jewel.* If you treated yourself like a priceless jewel on a daily basis, would you still be so inclined to make dark choices? Do this little experiment: treasure yourself as if you were a million pounds of gold, and then notice what happens in the outer world. Self-forgiveness is one of the most potent antidotes in existence for addressing the great pain in the heart of the world.

12

RETURNING
TO LOVE

In the absence of resentment, love flourishes. Love is naturally there. We don't have to generate love; we just have to clear away all the blocks that are in the way of our knowing our limitless, loving self. Most of us are trying so hard to be great—which is the ultimate irony, because greatness is who we are underneath our false personas. We were born great and need to allow ourselves to open back up to this fact. If we forgive our wounded selves, make peace with our past, and clean up the wreckage we've left in our wake, we will come face-to-face with the magnitude of all that we are. We will feel deep and unconditional love for ourselves—and not just love for the "good" parts of ourselves. When we step into the tranquil state of forgiveness, we feel genuine love of our whole self—the parts of us that are flawed and weak as well as those that are confident and strong.

Like turning on a light in a dark room, forgiveness brings the light of acceptance and compassion to all of our dark and disowned aspects. I can't remember the last person I worked with who, once they got in touch with the pain they had been hiding beneath their false persona, said, "Wow, I love my wounded ego!" Mostly we're embarrassed and horrified by it. There is a tendency for us to hate our false self, to sit in judgment on it, to be deeply ashamed of it and make it wrong. But our job is to see this part of ourselves from a new vantage point and find forgiveness for our wounded ego, which was driven by pain and desperation to construct a false persona and abandon all healthy boundaries.

Forgiveness allows us to see our wounded ego as the scared child that it is, trying with all its might to get approval. I hate to be so cliché as to use the term, but it is, in fact, *the wounded child within us* that needs our love. It needs our heartfelt appreciation and understanding. It needs to be reassured that if it comes out of hiding from behind our false persona, it will be loved and accepted with all its flaws and imperfections. Only when we have forgiven ourselves can we make this guarantee.

To move on and return to the self we were meant to be, we must commit to turning our lives over to a power greater than our smallest self. We must hand the reins back to the universe so that we can be used for exactly the purpose we have been put here for. It's so easy to think we are just one of 6 billion people and so we don't matter. But everything we do matters. Everything we say matters. Everything we think matters. Each of us is part of a collective heart that is a living organism. We have been delivered here to this earth with a gift, a special recipe that, if we allow it to unfold, will serve the greater whole.

The process of returning to our unified, limitless self is a holy one. It requires us to reunite with all of ourselves—all that we see, all that we can't see; all that there is, and all that will be. It demands that we give up our agendas, our self-righteous beliefs, and our will and surrender to a greater self, a self that exists beyond the individual and encompasses the collective heart—the good of all humanity. It demands that we face our shame, our sorrow, our regrets, and our pain and take responsibility for the human experience we have chosen, consciously or unconsciously, to live this lifetime. It demands that we give up our excuses and our self-pity, our denial and our projections, and be the person we deeply desire to be rather than exist as a small speck of our greater self. It requires us to stand in radical honesty, without judgment, and to view our lives from a spiritual perspective—through God's eyes rather than through our own. It requires us to heal the sores of our wounded egos and lay down the masks we have put on to protect ourselves from the pain of our broken hearts. To ensure we are on a path of love and safety, we must wake up to all that we are and all that we carry within us. We must take off the blinders that prevent us from seeing the vastness of both our humanity and our divinity.

Knowing the God of Our Hearts

In this human experience, most of us have learned to visit with God but not to know God. We learn to take some time on Saturday or Sunday to visit with God just as we would with our grandmother. Some of us put on our dress-up clothes to look nice for God, while others want to visit with God in the privacy of our own homes. But if we are to experience spiritual one-ness and transcendence, we must become aware of the deep human programming and the trance we are living in; otherwise, we will continue to look for spiritual soothing in all the wrong places. We will strive to find peace, fulfillment, love, and con-nection inside the structure of our limited minds and egos, and will be deeply disappointed to find that they don't exist inside our minds. God does not live in the mind, even though God has created the mind. God does not live in the individual con-sciousness of "you" or "me," although God exists there as well. God lives in the collective—in the vastness of this magnificent world. It is a presence not limited to a particular name or form. It is the truest, purest essence that resides within each of us. You can read all the scriptures and chant all the prayers, but if your heart is not connected to the collective whole, these acts have no essence, no meaning. Godly people can do ungodly things when the experience of God lives in their minds rather than in their hearts.

We do bad things when we think we are separate and alone and what we do doesn't matter. We do bad things when we are cut off from our divine essence and the grandness of our greater task here on earth. We do bad things when we are living only as a small speck of our greatest self, and we do bad things when we are hungry to return home to our spiritual core but won't allow ourselves to be nourished. We do bad things because we are disconnected, because we don't know any better, because we have separated and are trying desperately to get some unmet needs of the past met in ways that will never meet them anyway. The unmet need that can get met right now is the need to be whole, to be both your magnificent, divine self and your imperfect, human self.

The need that hungers for your attention and drives your every move whether you want to admit it or not is the need to explore your humanity and your divinity and come to rest in the vast, limitless self that you are. The need that will force you to commit unscrupulous acts of fraud and violence is only a diversion; it is a setup, and only you can stop yourself from falling into this trap. There is a hole there, and you can find it, admit to it, and seal it up with the divine energy that wants to come to you and through you. You, the big you, will never have true peace until the unification of both your light and your dark sides comes to fruition. And what better time is there than now? You can continue to point your finger at those who are doing much worse things than you in this lifetime, but that will lead you on a slow road to nowhere. For when you understand that you are both the victim and the victimizer, the prey and the predator, light and dark, good and bad, you will know yourself and others as the magical expressions of God that we all are. Then you can stop and observe. Then, rather than default to the voice of arrogance that says, "I would never do that or never be that," you have the choice to listen for the still, small voice within that quietly whispers, "There but for the Grace of God go I."

There is no quick fix. We live in an age of instant gratification, and I know this is not a popular stance. I know I should try to enroll you in the three easy steps to living a great life, but I can't, because to do so would be a lie. It takes work to live a great life. It takes work to know your inner world and the programming that has either led you to do bad things or put you in the path of others who are doing bad things. It takes constant care to ensure that you will live a purposeful life and feel fulfilled when you die. It takes courage to see and understand the implications and impact of your thoughts, words, and deeds.

It takes willingness to read the writing on the wall, to be vigilant enough with yourself to tell the truth, to be watchful for the signs that tell you when you are getting dangerously out of balance—when your dark side is about to act out.

Moving On

To move on and heal the shame that keeps you repeating destructive patterns, you must recognize that you are powerless to change the past. Holding on to your regrets, your hell-ridden dark memories, and your life-reducing guilt is just another way to kill off your spirit. It's another way to keep the cycle of shame and abuse alive. And I am here to ask you to stop. You don't deserve it, and you are the only one who can put an end to it. Even if you have done bad things in the past, if you are willing to take responsibility for your actions, learn from your mistakes, and find a way to make amends, you must let go of the guilt that drives you to do bad things.

Now is the time to wake up and separate from your shame body; to stop trying to avoid it—eat it away, drink it away, obsess it away, or fantasize it away—and instead make a conscious choice to do the opposite—go into it, feel it, learn from it, take responsibility for it—and move on. Now is the time to own up to what you need to be responsible for and what you have control over in the present and to recognize and compassionately acknowledge what has happened to you in the past that you had no control over.

If you allow what I'm saying to penetrate your walls of protection and denial, you can break through the lies of your shame body, your false self, and own up to what you have control over today. This is what you can do to break the cycle of abuse. And just in case you have forgotten: all self-sabotage is a form of abuse. It is abuse of the human spirit, of your innate right to be free from the bonds of your past, to stand tall and proud of who you are, all of you: your body, your mind, your sexuality—your entire self.

This is the time to fully grasp what you don't have control over (i.e., other people's behavior) and reclaim the power you do hold. This is the time to stop dwelling on what you can't change (what you did yesterday) and focus your attention on what you can do to heal your internal split, make peace with your past, and move on.

This is the time to focus on your own behavior. Most of you brave souls who are reading this book are probably reading it so that you can take care of someone else—your child, your spouse, a friend; or maybe you have been brutalized by someone else. It makes sense to a good person to focus on others, but you need to take care of you. You, me—all of us—must stop being in denial about who we are and our part in the breakdown of the human spirit and begin the process of minding our own business by seeing how we participate in the crimes against ourselves.

If you are reading this book because you know you are part of the problem, make the decision now to take back the power you have given to your false beliefs. Take back your power just for this day, and recognize that today you have power over the choices you make and the actions you take. You have the power to make life-altering decisions each day when you get out of bed. You have control over what you say to yourself when you look in the mirror and when you slip into the dark recesses of your shame body. You have the choice—when that little, wounded voice comes up and tells you that you are bad, disgusting, and wrong—to stop, take a breath, and say to your false self, "I hear your messages. I hear that you are alive, active, and in pain, but you are my wounded self, part of my false self—one aspect of my humanity that is here to support me in the evolution of my soul. You are the part of me that is here to wake me up and re-unite me with the vastness of my humanity and divinity. And I am going to send some love to you right now, because you are obviously deprived of love and acceptance or you wouldn't be acting this way." Yes, you have the ability to do this. You can understand cognitively that you are a well-programmed machine that has the power to make profound changes by taking life-affirming, self-respecting actions. You activate this power by taking back control and assuming responsibility for your life and your future. And if you need help because you are acting out in inappropriate ways, or if you can't stop yourself from hurting yourself and others, you have the power to get help. Snap yourself out of denial, humble yourself, let those around you know you need support, and find the help you need, right now. This might be your last chance.

Believe me, after leading Shadow Process retreats for over ten years around the world and coaching tens of thousands of people, I have heard every excuse, every rationalization, every justification and argument for why you should hold on to your bad behavior. But there is *no excuse* anymore. Stop it. Cut it out. The world needs you to return to your authentic expression; it needs you now.

You see, one of the lies of the false self is that you can't do anything about the dis-ease of your shame body—that you are powerless over your emotions and your shame-infested mind. But truth be told, you are not powerless over making the decision to heal your heart and make peace with your past. You might be powerless over an addiction, an obsession, or some other self-sabotaging behavior. But you are not powerless over asking for help.

All life-affirming choices change your inner dynamics. All of these actions are a sign of the power that lies within you. All of these choices show the wounded self that there is hope and that you do have some power. That is why you must make them. You must take back the reins from your shame body and the false persona you created to cover it up. You must confront the lies that drive your behavior so that you return to your rightful position—behind the wheel of your vehicle. You do not have to remain a helpless passenger who leaves the driving and direction of your life to a naive three-year-old or a wounded twelve-year-old. If you are not in charge of your future and the choices you make, who is? To whom have you turned your life over—a ghost from the past disguised as a voice in your mind?

I'm continually perplexed by all the reasons we find not to deal with what's shaping our lives. Could it be that difficult? Could it be that hard to stand up to the beliefs that haunt us day after day? Are we so beaten down that we don't have the strength or won't take the time to deal with internal demons that are now heading us in the wrong direction in some part of our lives? What has taken us over? When did it happen for you?

Growing up, I heard the Greyhound bus slogan over and over again: "Leave the driving to us." It was a great advertising campaign, but who wants to ride the bus these days? It is completely out of style, and unless you want a one-way ticket to a small town in the middle of nowhere (sorry to all you bus riders), you might want to take charge of the only vehicle you have, the only one that matters at the end of the day—yourself. You might want to get out of the passenger seat right now and get behind the wheel of your car. Unless you are willing to leave the driving to someone else (i.e., all the people who have added to your shame body and your unconscious internal map), you might want to set out on a new journey.

If you're not sure you're ready to make this change, just think about this: an incident that happened to you days, weeks, months, or years ago—a negative incident, something that caused you pain—now has the power to run you and ruin the rest of your life. Do you really want to let incidents from your past dictate the rest of your days on earth? Do you want your shame body to map out your future? Do you trust your pain to deliver you a great life—a life worth living?

I know; I can hear you all the way over here: "But I've tried. I can't do it. I'm stuck. It's not me who is the problem, it is my husband, wife, mother, boss, co-worker, accountant, brother, son . . . they did it to me." Yes, that is probably true on many levels. But now you are the one doing it to you. You are the one who is allowing old toxic shame to rob you of happiness, peace, and emotional freedom. You are the one who continuously shames yourself for your behaviors or the bad behaviors of others, and you are the only one who can stop it.

The only answer is love. Love all that you have hated. Love all that you have made wrong. Love all that is dark as well as all that is light. Love the human experience in all its complexity, and know that you and I are here for one reason only: to evolve our souls, to heal and transform our human selves, and to reconnect with the unlimited expression that opens up to us when we merge into the collective heart.

Pure Perfection

All of us are imperfect; all of us have made mistakes, said things we wish we hadn't, gotten trapped in an addiction, or put ourselves in front of an oncoming sabotage train and wished we had made another choice. Most of us can see the stupid things we have done and the very poor choices we have made, and most of us regret our poor judgment. But in order to ensure that we do not repeat the past, we must find the gifts of our bad behavior and poor choices and come to understand this one fundamental truth: everything we have done, everything we have experienced—every pain, every torment, and every struggle—is trying to teach us something and help us return to our highest expression and our authentic nature. Every fall from grace and self-destructive move is drenched in holiness—a gentle (or a not so gentle) nudge from our greatest self.

Understanding this truth will give you the wisdom to move on.

We are born in the image of our divine creator, pure and innocent, and then the human experience (i.e., the split) begins. Our human experiences blind us from seeing the perfection in the imperfection and from mining for the gold that eagerly awaits our discovery. What if today you realized that it is not only your good self that must be loved but your wounded self as well? What if you knew for certain that it is your suffering and your pain that can lead you to living a life of goodness, virtue, and self-respect? I am here to tell you that it is the very thing that you despise and don't want to be that can help you become the person you always wanted to be.

It was my weakness and suffering from addiction that brought me to my knees and opened me up to greater realities. Arrogance is what made me believe I knew more than most people, and it was ignorance that made me get down on my knees every night for years and beg God for spiritual wisdom and new ways to integrate my emotional pain. My fear of being called lazy gives me my drive. It is my vanity that dresses me in the morning and gets me to work out even when I'm tired. My fear of being a negligent mother makes sure that I go to all the flag football games (even when I'm busy) and drive my son to school (even when I'm tired and he could take the bus). It is my greed and love for fine things that drive me to work when others are out partying, and it is my denial of the evil and angry judgments of others that allows me to stand up in front of group after group and tout my message—to heal the split between the two forces that exist within each of us. And it is my depressive nature that birthed the Pollyanna in me that relentlessly tries to transform the untransformable and never gives up hope on the hopeless.

My feelings of inadequacy have me wake up in the morning and ask what can I do to make my world a better place. My need to matter, to be all used up when I die, was birthed out of the fear that I, Deborah Sue Ford, would die unnoticed, that

I would be nothing more than a middle-class Jewish girl from Hollywood, Florida.

So I invite you to put away your judgments, lay down the boxing gloves that keep you fighting, and surrender to the love you are looking for. That love lives inside you. When properly dispensed, it will heal your greatest sorrow and wipe away your regrets. It will soothe your soul and nurture your aching heart. It will shine its light where there is darkness and lead you out of the darkness and into the light—the light of love—where the collective heart awaits your return.

ACKNOWLEDGMENTS

To Gideon Weil, my editor, I could never have written this book without your brilliant insights, vision, and coaching. And to Danielle Dorman, Debra Evans, and Frankie Mazon for the enormous contribution that you each made. This book would not have been possible without you.

To read all of my acknowledgments, visit
www.DebbieFord.com/acknowledgments.

ABOUT THE AUTHOR

Debbie Ford, the creator of the renowned Shadow Process Workshop, is a pioneering force in incorporating the study and integration of the shadow into modern psychological and spiritual practices. The foremost expert on emotional education, she is the founder of the Ford Institute for Integrative Coaching at JFK University, offering virtual training programs to students around the world. A sought-after speaker and teacher, Debbie was recently featured on an ABC TV series and is also the host of her own radio show.

Passionate about education, Debbie and her community of coaches founded **The Global Heart of Integrative Coaching,** a nonprofit organization committed to building schools and bringing transformational skills to communities worldwide. Visit www.theglobalheart.org.

To learn more about Debbie's life-changing books, audio programs, workshops, trainings, and radio show, or to hire a coach, please visit www. DebbieFord.com.

In an effort to end the abuse of women, a portion of the proceeds of *Why Good People Do Bad Things* is going to support women worldwide.